# Lighter as We Go

# Lighter as We Go

*Virtues, Character Strengths, and Aging*

Mindy Greenstein

Jimmie Holland

**OXFORD**
UNIVERSITY PRESS

# OXFORD
UNIVERSITY PRESS

Oxford University Press is a department of the University of
Oxford. It furthers the University's objective of excellence in research,
scholarship, and education by publishing worldwide.

Oxford   New York

Auckland   Cape Town   Dar es Salaam   Hong Kong   Karachi
Kuala Lumpur   Madrid   Melbourne   Mexico City   Nairobi
New Delhi   Shanghai   Taipei   Toronto

With offices in

Argentina   Austria   Brazil   Chile   Czech Republic   France   Greece
Guatemala   Hungary   Italy   Japan   Poland   Portugal   Singapore
South Korea   Switzerland   Thailand   Turkey   Ukraine   Vietnam

Oxford is a registered trademark of Oxford University Press
in the UK and certain other countries.

Published in the United States of America by
Oxford University Press
198 Madison Avenue, New York, NY 10016

© Mindy Greenstein and Jimmie Holland 2015

Library of Congress Cataloging-in-Publication Data
Greenstein, Mindy.
Lighter as we go : virtues, character strengths, and aging / Mindy Greenstein,
Jimmie Holland.
pages cm
Includes bibliographical references and index.
ISBN 978–0–19–936095–6 (hardback)
1.  Aging—Social aspects. 2.  Aging—Psychological aspects. 3.  Well-being—
Age factors. 4.  Middle age—Psychological aspects. 5.  Middle age—Social aspects.
6.  Older people—Psychology. I. Holland, Jimmie. II. Title.
HQ1061.G717 2014
305.260973—dc23
2014007924

3 5 7 9 8 6 4
Printed in the United States of America
on acid-free paper

*Mindy Greenstein: For Rob, Max, and Isaac. Always.*
*Jimmie Holland: For my grandchildren with love, Jennifer, Madeline,*
*Delia, Andy, Elizabeth, Jimmy, Daniel, Owen, and Lilly, and in*
*memory of Gabriel.*

*Older adults constitute the only increasing natural resource in the entire world.*
—Linda Fried
Dean, Columbia School of Public Health

# Contents

# Acknowledgments

We thank Marguerite Lederberg, wise colleague; Madeline Holland, scholarly granddaughter and midwife to the Vintage Readers Book Club; Demece Garepis, daughter-in-law with tech expertise to get Jimmie through; Errol Philip, for the technological expertise to get Mindy through; Daniel Garepis-Holland, for the Grandma Software program; Max and Isaac, for teaching Mindy to see the world through their young eyes; Ivelisse Belardo, the kind and resourceful keeper of Jimmie's head; Talia Weiss, remarkably effective research assistant; Zaneta McMichael, keeper of the Aging and Illness support group and Vintage Readers Book Club; colleagues, Chris Nelson, Andy Roth, Liz Harvey, William Breitbart, and Yesne Alici; the Vintage Readers and Aging and Illness group members, for their stimulating discussions and remarkable insights; all the men and women who shared their stories and hard earned wisdom, including family and friends who participated in long surveys or interviews; the many people who supported our project through the years; and our husbands, Rob and Jim, who are always there to support us.

# Introduction

*So many of us start dreading age when we are in high school.*
*I think that is really a waste of a lovely life.*
—Betty White, actress, 90

This was a year of big round birthdays for both of us.

At 85, Jimmie is now at the age known as the "old old" and, like most, wonders how it all happened so fast. As a child, she always enjoyed talking to the "old folks" and she loved hearing her mother and aunts laugh about the "good old days." She loves history and lives in a house that was once commandeered by Sir William Howe as headquarters when he fought George Washington across the Bronx River in the Battle of White Plains. No wonder Jimmie's favorite mystery is *The Spy* by James Fenimore Cooper. She feels a deep sense of gratitude to have lived so long in good health and feels life has been good, and still is. That's why the friends who attended her eighty-fifth birthday bash got a refrigerator magnet that announced, "It-is-better-than-you-think."

Mindy's big birthday this year was her fiftieth. As it approached, she was reminded of an experience she'd had a few years earlier. It was a bright June day, and Mindy, 43 at the time, was walking down Riverside Drive in her neighborhood in New York City. She normally moved at a brisk pace, but, this time, she was stuck behind two women who were moving very slowly. One of them looked to be in her late 80s or maybe 90s. She was small and frail and was leaning heavily on her walker, the kind with tennis balls squeezed around the bottoms of its legs to make them glide more easily. The woman chatted comfortably with her younger companion, but it was taking them a very long time even to get to the corner of the block. Mindy waited for the right unobtrusive moment to move ahead. She felt bad for the older woman. How awful it must be to have to work so hard and so long just to walk a couple of blocks.

Just one week later, Mindy was diagnosed with breast cancer. Suddenly, she couldn't even be sure she'd make it to 50, let alone 80 or 90. And she thought, "Oh, to be that lucky woman, and know I made it that far!" Who cared how long it might take to walk a couple of blocks? When she turned 50 this year, she didn't fret about getting older, she celebrated it. And one way she celebrated was by working on this book with Jimmie during weekly meetings.

From our different vantage points, we can both see how much society needs an attitude adjustment when it comes to aging. There's an old saying that "aging sucks, but it beats the alternative." Both of us have seen some of those alternatives up close and in more ways than one, and they have given us a unique perspective on just how much it beats the alternative. We don't claim that aging is all good, but it certainly isn't all bad. Like any other time of life, being older is a mix of both. Besides, as we'll discuss, a great deal of social science research suggests that many people experience life in older age in a much more positive way than first thought. More positive, even, than when they were younger.

These data on well-being through the lifespan gave rise to the idea of the "U-bend of life," named for the U-shaped curve researchers found: our sense of well-being starts out high in young adulthood, then goes down, plateauing in middle age, and then goes right back up again, and keeps going up through our 70s, 80s, and beyond. Over time, we learn how to see things in greater perspective. In the words of philosopher William May, we learn to "travel light."

But, too often, the negative stereotypes scare the young and make elders feel worse about themselves. Mid-lifers fear becoming old, and young adults fear becoming midlifers (they can barely conceive of being Jimmie's age), like one long cascading domino effect of the fears of aging. Even the term *aging* is a matter of perspective. When Mindy first suggested that aging scares not only younger people but also middle-aged people like herself, Jimmie smiled and said, "But, Mindy, you are younger people!"

So, how did we come to work together to write *Lighter as We Go*?

Both of us have extensive experience talking with people of all ages who are facing a possibly shortened life span. Jimmie is a psychiatrist who has always been fascinated by how people face serious life challenges. She went to Memorial Sloan-Kettering Cancer Center in 1977 to start the first psychological and psychiatric services in a cancer center, a dimension of care that had been woefully neglected. She founded and nurtured the field of psycho-oncology (a subspecialty of oncology), developing world-renowned clinical and research programs, as well as training programs for the next generation of psycho-oncologists. The success of her efforts led to the development of similar services in cancer centers around the world and to a mandate by the Institute of Medicine that cancer treatment programs incorporate ways of caring for the mind as well as the body.

She has personally helped hundreds of patients cope with the existential crisis of serious illness.

Mindy, a clinical psychologist, went to Memorial in the late 1990s to train as a psycho-oncologist in Jimmie's department. During her two years as a fellow, she served as the psychiatry service's chief clinical fellow in 1998 and as one of the developers of Meaning-Centered Group Psychotherapy, an intervention to help people with cancer find meaning in their lives. She has also worked with many men and women who were dealing with the existential crisis of a cancer diagnosis and the potential losses it brings.

Around 2005, a new challenge emerged at Memorial: the rapidly growing elder population who developed cancer, and the inadequate attention to helping them deal with the unique combination of issues they faced. They were already dealing with losses of spouse, peers, diminished vision, hearing, and mobility—the added burden of illness and treatment seemed too much. Yet, there were virtually no support services developed with elders in mind.

Jimmie, then in her 70s, started a multidisciplinary geriatric psychiatry team to develop a supportive counseling program for older patients along with Dr. Andy Roth, a psychiatrist, Dr. Chris Nelson, a psychologist, Anne Martin, a social worker, and Liz Harvey, a counselor. Mindy joined the team after her own cancer treatment and with her newfound appreciation for the positive aspects of aging. The team also engaged the help of the real experts—the men and women aged 70 and older who had faced cancer and were eager to give informed opinions. They were not shy in telling us when we were dead wrong—or occasionally right. One outcome of our efforts was our biweekly Aging and Illness support group, where new questions and innovations can be explored with the patient experts.

And what did the elders talk about? Their primary beef was, "I hate the words that elders get called," like "geezer," "codger," "coot," "old lady," "pops," and "out to pasture." Jimmie remembered her own mother's complaints long ago about "senior citizen"—"Show me a junior citizen, first!" Velma would say. They sometimes felt demeaned by the unkind or condescending things people sometimes said to them. We asked what they would prefer to be called. One octogenarian member, Eddie Weaver, suggested "seasoned elders," which the group found far preferable.

One question that came up was whether these ageist attitudes were a product of modern society and its romance with youth and beauty or had it been around in earlier cultures? Learning the answer to that question turned out to be an intergenerational effort, spurred by the love of a granddaughter and grandmother.

Jimmie and her granddaughter, Madeline, started their own grandmother–granddaughter book club during Madeline's gap year before college. They were reading the Harvard 50 Classics of World Literature together and enjoying their discussions immensely. When Madeline started school and had to stop their book club, she suggested that it could be an equally exciting activity for the Aging and Illness group, especially those who were home alone a lot. The group was enthusiastic about the idea, and the Vintage Readers Book Club was born in the spring of 2012. The book club has grown even more popular than the group that spawned it.

A 93-year-old Vintage Reader chose Cicero's *Essay on Old Age* from 44 BC as the second reading. To everyone's surprise, Cicero quickly answered our question: the same ageist attitudes were writ large in Roman antiquity more than 2,000 years ago. And as we'll see in chapter 4, in which we discuss the history of older age, so were some of their antidotes. The group had to agree with Cicero that they were far from morose or sitting around twiddling their thumbs awaiting death, as younger people often assumed. Instead, they were very engaged with life, living in the now, and sharing how-do-you-do-it's with each other, especially in the group.

Whether in the Aging and Illness group or the Vintage Readers Book Club, we found our discussions of aging illuminating. Past and present melded, as group members described how they coped with life, using "old-fashioned" terms like *love*, *courage*, and *kindness*, words harkening back to the original virtues, or character strengths, as described by the ancient Greeks and repeated in the world's great philosophical and religious traditions. It was through these virtues and character strengths that they had learned to *travel light*.

At the same time, *traveling light* helped them develop those strengths further. When they told their life stories, they used the virtues to describe not only their joys but also how they faced the rough times. They told funny stories and sad ones, as they might have at any other point in their lives. They told them with humor, humility, and the sense that they did the best they could, given the hand they were dealt. Even though all had some regrets, they would want to repeat the same life, or as Ben Franklin put it—in our first book club reading—"were it offered to my choice, I should have no objection to a repetition of the same life from its beginning, only asking the advantages authors have in a second edition to correct some faults of the first" (1).

There is a big disconnect between beliefs about aging and the reality as expressed by many older people who say it is not as grim as advertised and that there are gains that go unappreciated (though it is easy, of course, to find exceptions). A large reason for this disconnect is that we often have too little interaction with the members of different generations. *Lighter as We Go* is meant for adults of all ages, as it is written by women spanning two generations (and informed by a third generation—Madeline contributed not only her insights about her own young age but about early drafts of the book as well). We explore the experience of aging in general, focusing on middle and older age, in light of what we've learned from people we have met with individually or in groups, some exciting new avenues in medical and psychological research, history, books and movies, stories about people's day-to-day lives, and our own personal and clinical perspectives.

The two of us have so enjoyed exploring this terrain together. And Mindy has the added benefit of seeing up close the example of aging that Jimmie sets (even though Jimmie is quick to remind her not to idealize her simply because she's older). We hope *Lighter as We Go* inspires similar intergenerational dialogues about life's challenges and joys. A book about aging isn't necessarily about aging at all. It's about living and about how we cope and thrive throughout our lives.

## REFERENCES

Cicero, M. T. (1820). *An Essay on Old Age*. Translated by W. Melmoth. Google Ebook.

Franklin, B. (1961). *The Autobiography and Other Writings*. New York: Penguin.

May, W. (1986). The virtues and vices of the elderly. In T. R. Cole and S.A. Gadow (eds.), *What Does it Mean to Grow Old: Reflections from the Humanities*. Durham: Duke University Press.

# Part I

# Character, Character Strength, and Continuity Over Time

# 1

# The Oak Tree and the U-Bend

## Age, Well-Being, and the Experience of *Me*'ness

*What is it that persists and endures?*
—James Hillman, *The Force of Character*

### THE OAK TREE

One of the particular challenges we face in life is in developing our sense of identity over time, as it both changes and stays constant. For instance, the younger person may ask, *Who am I?* as she navigates the development of her career path or relationships with significant others. On the other hand, author Mary Catherine Bateson suggests that the older person may ask, instead, *Am I still the person I have spent a lifetime becoming?* as she deals with changes in her physical experiences, career trajectory, or any of the other changes that come with moving on in life. *How do I grow older and remain myself,* we wonder as time passes, *or rather, how, in growing older, do I become more truly myself?* (Bateson, p. 237).

Throughout all this developing—call it aging or growing—there is a *me* that continues, changing and growing more nuanced, but still *me*. At age 50, Mindy is still the Mindy in her kindergarten picture from P.S. 52. She is still that little girl in some sense, even though her life is nothing like she imagined it would be—and she looks both different (a few more lines on her face, darker hair, less visibly afraid of the world) and the same (still the shortest one in the room, same high'ish cheekbones, same smirky smile).

At age 85, Jimmie is still Jimmie. She still feels like a country girl who has no idea how she got from Nevada, Texas, to the big city, but it has been a great adventure and she wouldn't change it or do it over in any other way. She, too, has some more lines on her face but hasn't quite lost what a friend once called her Linda Darnell (a popular 1940s movie star) look, especially when she smiles. As one elder once told us, "I'm still *me*, only more so!"

So, what is this *me*? At its core is what, in the old days, we used to call character. Character is both stable and continually developing over time. For example, Nelson Mandela in his youth was the leader of the African National Congress's armed wing. Yet, in his elder years, he was the man who helped bring and maintain peace between the angry factions on both sides. He didn't change into someone else between those times. Rather, his sense of *me* grew over the years, as his life circumstances changed and as he learned the ways in which he himself could help to further change those circumstances.

The term *character* fell out of use as psychiatry and behavioral science became enthralled with the pathological side of personality. The psychologist James Hillman went so far as to lament, "Character died in the twentieth century. . .

becoming irrelevant to philosophy and science" (165). But he hoped to fix that with his lyric descriptions of it:

*What ages is not merely your functions and organs, but the whole of your nature, that particular person you have come to be and already were years ago. Character has been forming your face, your habits, your friendships, your peculiarities, the level of your ambition with its career and its faults. Character influences the way you give and receive; it affects your loves and your children. It walks you home at night and can keep you long awake.* (xv)

Anthropologist Sharon Kaufman (1986) describes this sense of *me*'ness as "the ageless self." She thinks of it as the story we put together of our lives over time, in which certain themes or patterns emerge, giving our present life a sense of continuity and coherence with the past.

## Lillian and Linda: What Stays the Same

Lillian Deutsch, an intellectual 90-year-old woman with strong political opinions, feels both the same as and different than her younger self. Her left-leaning views have not changed or softened over the years and neither has her general philosophy on life. Intellect and education were always foremost to her, and she prided herself on the high standards she kept, both for others and for herself. What's changed is the context. Unfortunately, most of her friends with similar political views have died, and so Lillian finds herself choosing between sparring with others over her views or keeping silent. She finds fewer opportunities for conversation with like-minded people, which causes her to feel lonely. But she maintains her sense of pride in sticking to her guns and staying engaged with current events.

Linda Moore, a writer in her 60s, is still the same persistent, conscientious woman who likes to work creatively and use her imagination, as when she was younger. What's changed for her is that she now more readily accepts that she can't reach all her goals. With that change, she experiences a sense of peace that she didn't have years before, even though she may still strive for many of the same things.

Bateson thinks of growing into the older versions of ourselves as an improvisational art form that calls for "imagination and a willingness to learn." An open mind to deal with repeated changes is critical, but it must be coupled with a firm grip on "what is essential to one's identity." Hillman likens the process, in one particularly beautiful passage, to the relationship between the acorn and the oak tree.

At birth, character barely exists, it's about the size of a tiny acorn, then it begins to grow. You begin to hear comments that a child has a particular characteristic: "Isn't that just like Donny to be so generous" or "Jane is always thoughtful of her sister." The oak's trunk grows bigger and sturdier and begins to put out branches. Similarly, character develops like limbs on the tree. Each new developmental task both requires and nurtures the development of character strengths: courage to view self separate from parents; self-control to hold a job and behave ethically; humanity to allow mature intimacy with another; trying to be a wise parent.

As the years go by, the oak becomes bigger, sturdier, with more branches sprouting in older age as more challenges are met: one for reaching maturity; one for teaching the younger generation; one for caring for elderly parents; one for adapting to losses of peers and family; one for tolerating the physical changes that come with aging. All the while, the person remains the same person, just as the growing tree remains the same tree. The new "branches"—and developing strengths of character—declare, "I am still me," despite all the losses and change. By the end of a long life, the result is a mighty oak that has withstood ravages confronted over the course of a long life. Hillman noted that it takes a lot of living to develop character, and it only emerges in its fullness in elders: "How we age, the patterns we regularly perform, and the style of our image show character at work. As character directs aging, aging reveals character" (Hillman, xviii).

In their identity balance theory, psychologists Joel Sneed and Susan Whitbourne (2005) suggest two processes that help us keep a balanced sense of who we are, even as we grow and change in appearance over the years. For example, one thing that changes for everyone is our sense of competence at various tasks. We might get better at some tasks over time. For instance, our verbal memory and vocabulary tend to get better during middle age, whereas our speed tends to start dipping compared with our speed ten years earlier. When we have an experience that challenges our sense of competency—say, losing a race you used to win handily—you might respond with identity assimilation, that is, you'd seek information that's consistent with your current image of yourself and minimize the importance of the change. Perhaps, you lost the race because you were just having an off day, or hadn't gotten enough sleep the night before, or hadn't broken in your new running shoes well enough.

But if you keep losing races, start getting winded more easily than you used to, or face some insurmountable obstacle, like consequences of a serious illness, you're more likely to start modifying your idea of who you are and what you can do. This is called identity accommodation, and it can be both positive and negative. On the one hand, you might be sad to think of yourself as less competent at some activities. On the other, you may think of yourself as more competent at other things and experience these changes as personal growth, rather than as losing something.

The idea of identity balance comes from the fact that not every new experience leads to changing your fundamental assumptions about how you define yourself. You're still you, just a version that gets more easily winded on the stairs. And even when major changes are made, there is still a core identity underlying those changes.

Perhaps, identities of professional athletes seem more sensitive to forced change because of physical changes. Even in these cases, however, there are gradations that might allow for more identity balance than one might think: the retired athlete might stay athletic and play for fun instead of for a living. He might move into a managerial, executive, or commentator position within the athletic area or use some skills he'd honed over the years to go into business.

### Bob Feller

Bob Feller, the legendary Cleveland Indians pitcher—it was estimated that he could throw a

104-mile-per-hour fastball—retired in 1956 after decades as one of the most famous pitchers in the major leagues. He then built a successful insurance business, got a pilot's license, and returned every year to tutor the Cleveland Indians' pitching staff (Orr, 2010). While some aspects of his identity changed over the years, other core aspects stayed the same, and he could experience himself as a coherent whole, despite all the changes.

To understand the concept of character, we need also to understand the concept of character strength. It is the strengths, or virtues as the ancient Greeks referred to them, that act as the better or, more adaptive, part of our nature. We rely on these strengths to counter the worst parts of our nature, our vices, our excesses, our thoughtlessness. The philosopher Sissela Bok suggests that character strengths serve an important evolutionary function; they are an internal mechanism for controlling our behavior so that cultures can flourish and grow. Without them, society would be vulnerable to self-destructive behaviors. Bok argues, "Certain moral values go to the heart of what it means to be human. . . and always must if we are not to lose touch with our humanity" (cited in Peterson and Seligman, 33).

Our character strengths often develop as we live (or muddle) through crises but also simply as we live through various experiences over time. Sometimes we take pride in our character; sometimes, we disappoint ourselves. Both the pride and the disappointment teach us and give us direction about how to handle future challenges. The longer we're around, the more data we have, the more chances we have to get things "right," not by someone else's external measure, but by our own moral or psychological compass.

The virtues we will discuss are those aspects of character that are nurtured through both our successes and our failures and that we feel represent the best in us. Over time, we realize that we might actually like this *me*, that it has learned a thing or two about life along the way, and that it might be worth sharing those things with others a few years behind us. And, that *me* might even be sturdy enough to allow us to admit that we might also learn a thing or two from those younger—and older. Perhaps, most important, is that this sense of *me*'ness is always there as long as we're around (and even afterward, in the memories we leave behind), the way an oak stays in its place but gets stronger and sturdier and keeps growing more interesting the older it gets.

Character strengths may be at the heart of a fascinating phenomenon that consistently finds its way into the research literature on well-being through the lifespan, the U-Bend of Life.

## THE U-BEND

As we mentioned in our introduction, research has shown that among people between the ages of 18 and 85, the age group that feels the greatest sense of well-being is 82–85. If you were surprised to learn that, so were the social scientists who kept finding, again and again—even in different countries—that despite the common perception that aging is something to be feared, well-being actually went up in older age rather than down. Even more interesting, researcher Arthur Stone and his colleagues (2010) analyzed a 2008 US

Gallup poll of more than 340,000 people who were asked to rate their general sense of well-being on a scale from 0 to 10, where 0 represented "the worst possible life for you" and 10 represented "the best possible life for you."

Figure 1.1 shows the U-shaped curve that Stone and others found. At age 18, feelings of well-being and enjoyment of life are pretty high (a little more than 6.8 on the scale). No great surprise there, but what did surprise various researchers who kept getting similar results was that those feelings of well-being quickly started to go down over the following years, reaching bottom around the early 50s. After that came another surprise. Feelings of well-being started to climb right back up and continued to climb the older the individuals got, with 82- to 85-year-olds scoring even higher than 18-year-olds. This U-bend of well-being has been found over and over again. The oldest subjects studied to date were 88, and the trend continued. Some studies suggest the pattern holds even for elders who complain of both cognitive and physical decline, though these

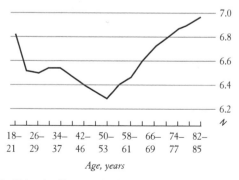

**Figure 1.1** The U-bend: self-reported well-being, on a scale of 1–10
Copyright The Economist Newspaper Limited, London (December 16, 2010)

counterintuitive findings are the subject of continued study in order to understand why.

In 2008, Blanchflower and Oswald looked at the data on the U-bend from all over the world. Depending on the study, subjects were asked the following: "Taken together, how would you say things are these days—would you say that you are happy, pretty happy, or not too happy?" or "On the whole, are you very satisfied, fairly satisfied, not very satisfied, or not at all satisfied with the life you lead?"

They found the same U-shaped curve in 500,000 Americans and Western Europeans, as well as in individuals from Eastern Europe, Latin America, and Asian countries; their data included 72 developed and developing countries. Blanchflower and Oswald looked into the possibility that the actual time period when people were born might explain the results, rather than their ages; this is known as a cohort effect. However, they found that the data were due to age.

In addition, Stone and colleagues (2010) asked individuals about specific feelings, such as enjoyment, happiness, and stress. Most of these feelings showed a similar relationship to age, with positive feelings starting high in early adulthood, going down through middle age, and going back up with older age; negative feelings did the opposite. One interesting exception is in the case of stress, which actually increased when subjects were in their early 20s, then went down thereafter, and kept going down in their middle and older years.

Of course, it's important to acknowledge that not everyone fits the profile that researchers found. These data are aggregate statistics, referring to people in general, not to everyone. It is easy to think of startling examples of individuals who do not fit this cheery picture. We'll discuss some of the issues related to the ways in which life might actually get *heavier* over time in chapter 12. In general, though, the research does seem to confirm that for many people, *life gets lighter*.

So, what might be going on and, more important, what can we all learn from it? The question is more than theoretical. According to a 2009 study by Becca Levy and her colleagues at Yale University, people who have negative stereotypes of aging when they're young are more likely to have serious chronic diseases as they get older compared with individuals with a more positive view of aging. One possible explanation, which we'll explore further in chapter 9, is a self-fulfilling prophecy; people with more positive expectations about older age might be more likely to develop healthier habits. These data suggest one reason why it's important to help younger people be less afraid of aging: the better their view of aging, the more invested they might be now in developing the habits that will make their older age more pleasant.

We had to ask ourselves, "What is it that happens over the course of our lives that enables us to feel better over time, when most of us assume we're going to feel worse?" And what does the answer mean for how we might live our lives now, regardless of our age? Before we can understand the role that individual character strengths might play in all this, let's first consider how we generally experience life throughout our adult lives.

## REFERENCES

Bateson, M. C. (2010). *Composing a Further Life: The Age of Active Wisdom*. New York: Alfred A. Knopf.

Blanchflower, D. G., & Oswald, A. J. (2008). Is well-being U-shaped over the life cycle? *Soc Sci Med*, *66*(8), 1733–1749. doi:10.1016/j.socscimed.2008.01.030

Bok, S. (1995). *Common Values*. Columbia, Mo.: University of Missouri Press.

*Economist*. (2010). The U-bend of life: Why, beyond middle age, people get happier as they get older. *The Economist*, 33–36.

Hillman, J. (2000). *The Force of Character and the Lasting Life*. New York: Ballantine Books.

Kaufman, S. R. (1986). *The Ageless Self: Sources and Meaning in Late Life*. Madison, Wis.: University of Wiconsin Press.

Levy, B. R., Zonderman, A. B., Slade, M. D., & Ferrucci, L. (2009). Age stereotypes held earlier in life predict cardio-vascular events in later life. *Psychol Sci*, *20*(3), 296–298. doi:10.1111/j.1467-9280.2009.02298.x

Orr, M. (2010, December 15, 2010). Last Word: Bob Feller. *The New York Times*. Retrieved from http://www.nytimes.com/video/obituaries/1247464008751/last-word-bob-feller.html

Peterson, C., & Seligman, M. (2004). *Character Strengths and Virtues: Handbook and Classification:* New York/Washington, D.C.: American Psychological Association/Oxford University Press.

Sneed, J. R., & Whitbourne, S. K. (2005). Models of the aging self. *J Soc Issues*, *61*(2), 375–388.

Stone, A. A., Schwartz, J. E., Broderick, J. E., & Deaton, A. (2010). A snapshot of the age distribution of psychological well-being in the United States. *Proc Natl Acad Sci U S A 107*(22), 9985–9990. doi:10.1073/pnas.1003744107

# 2

# A Look at the Grownup Years

Early, Middle, and Later Adulthood

Young adults "dwell in possibility" and feel like the engine of their own actions. If they want to go out dancing until the middle of the night, there's no one to tell them not to, no children they have to get home to. Old enough that their parents are no longer looking over their shoulders daily, but young enough that many choices are still open for them to explore and they can enjoy many different areas of life. They don't think about aging or mortality. As Kate, a 75-year-old retired psychiatrist and colleague, looks back to that time of her life, she laughs, "I was too busy living to think about older age!"

Jimmie's 22-year-old granddaughter, Madeline, who is in this age group, is very aware of all that's open to her as a result. "We don't think about aging," she says, "but we're aware of our youth, and bask in it." It would be hard not to bask, of course, in such a famously youth-oriented culture, with movies, television shows, and advertising all geared toward Madeline and her peers. The *New Yorker*, for instance, publishes a yearly "30 Under 30" issue, making it a point to highlight young writers. When was the last time they ran one titled "40 Over 40" or "50 Over 50"?

Madeline and her friends live in the now, exploring different interests. But, as she points out, it's hardly all fun and games. Being young also brings with it a paradoxical challenge—while they might not be aware of the finiteness of life, they're certainly aware of the finiteness of youth. And they feel a sense of urgency to take advantage of that youth before the full responsibilities of adulthood set in. Young adults fear the idea of looking back one day and regretting the things they didn't do.

This tension is consistent with one of the interesting findings of the U-bend research, namely, that stress is at its highest when we're in our early 20s, before it starts its lifelong descent. Madeline tells us about a popular teen acronym—YOLO—You Only Live Once. It's their motto, sometimes used as an excuse for the rash misadventures teens and young adults are famous for. In other words, the future is something to be feared, so you'd better live in the now *now*, before life takes away your chance to enjoy it later (and they haven't even seen the U-bend dip!). Deborah, now 60, remembers that age well. "I thought I would never get to laugh anymore once I got older." Of course, she laughs about that thought now, but she took it very seriously back in the day.

There is an anxiety implicit in what otherwise sounds like a wonderfully liberating time of life—having the ability to explore who you are and what you want also implies that you don't yet enjoy the stability of having an identity or a sense of what path you want to take in life. And the enjoyment of "the now" also includes a sense of apprehension about the future, one that equates aging with becoming less active, less in control of what you get to do in life. Ironically, learning more about the U-bend and the possibility that the long-term future actually holds something positive might alleviate the stresses of those early years—helping younger adults enjoy the now, free of the fear that they won't be able to enjoy what comes later, as well.

As Madeline and her friends grow (they never age, she says, only grow), they will start to learn who they are through the choices they make and how they react to whatever life throws at them. They'll start taking on the responsibilities that they were brought up to expect—making a living, finding a life partner, perhaps raising children. Rather than living in the now, this next part of adulthood will involve greater explicit thinking about future goals, whether in the guise of working toward career goals or raising children and helping them reach their goals. At the same time, their children will remind them of their own pasts, what they used to do and think at the same age.

Life becomes more complicated when we're in our 30s and 40s, as decisions made earlier in life now become more concrete and less open to changes than before. At this point, we come to grips with goals reached—and those that are likely not reachable.

## THE SANDWICH YEARS

When Madeline becomes middle-aged, she'll enter Mindy's territory. Having just turned 50, Mindy is unfortunately at the bottom of the U-bend curve. But, with a downside is always an upside—in this case, literally; according to the data, her sense of well-being has nowhere to go but up.

Let's take a look from a psychological standpoint at why this might happen.

If life were *The Brady Bunch*—a television show known to many of Mindy's generation—we middle-agers would be Jan, the middle child; less interesting than Marcia, the eldest; not as cute as Cindy, the youngest. For many years, even researchers thought that nothing interesting happened in midlife, and data were sparse. Fortunately, that has changed, especially thanks to the MacArthur Midlife in the United States (MIDUS) fellowship grant from the mid-1990s. The grant was established to study the way we actually experience middle age in the United States.

Before the MIDUS grant, developmental psychologist Erik Erikson (1950) was the first to even suggest that there was any development after childhood. He theorized that midlife was the time when our life task is generativity— literally, to generate. Whether it's children (or protégés), ideas, or products, we generate and nurture. While raising the next generation of children, we also influence the next generation of colleagues and neighbors, either actively, through mentoring, or passively, by example. We nurture not only people and ideas but also institutions. Psychiatrist George Vaillant refers to us as society's "keepers of meaning," a role we will continue into older age.

## Nancy Miller, 63-year-old Retired Engineer

"People over 60 have less to lose," Nancy feels. "Their striving is over, and now you can take risks. It's a time to be generative. You have to go out of your way to connect with people." Nancy has been actively try-ing to do just that and is interested in working with museums and libraries to organize conferences on topics in philosophy and science that anyone of any age might find interesting.

Navigating these very important multiple roles can be extremely challenging. In "The Virtues and Vices of the Elderly," ethicist William May describes the plight of midlifers like Mindy, who "perceive themselves as fortresses beleaguered on different fronts by aging parents and wayward adolescents" (58). He's got a point.

### Mindy, Last Year (Age 49 at the Time)

I was supposed to discuss the sandwichers' experience on a panel about aging. But I couldn't make it at the last minute: my mother had just had an exacerbation of chronic obstructive pulmonary disease (COPD), and was on a respirator in the intensive care unit of a Brooklyn hospital, at the same time that my 15-year-old son, Max, needed a medical procedure at a hospital in uptown Manhattan. At exactly the moment I was to have given my talk, I was deciding how long to stay with my husband at Max's bedside, while he recovered from his endoscopy, before I hopped on a train to Brooklyn to visit my mother, who might or might not be able to come off her respirator.

I informed the moderator and we both had to laugh. All the moderator had to do was tell the audience why I couldn't make it and that could stand by itself as my entire presentation. As one midlifer once told me, when stress is particularly high, the "sandwich years" easily feel like the "panini years." (My mother did eventually come off her respirator, but my daily Manhattan–Brooklyn hustle would last for a couple of months.)

Midway between past and future, midlifers have an interesting experience of time. If we have children, we're particularly aware of time passing as we watch them grow. If we have elderly parents, we are particularly aware of their time passing. Concerns about aging start coming to the fore. Often, those concerns are accompanied by a sense of dread, which may contribute to the U-bend finding that our sense of well-being is lowest in our early 50s. (Perhaps knowing that well-being will often go up as we get older will add a dose of optimism to that dread!)

In addition, it's the middle years when we become more acquainted with mortality, ours and everyone else's. Some friends (or we ourselves) will become sick. We're not as fast as we used to be at basketball or tennis. Aches and pains start to set in. Flab starts to poke out of new places. Elderly parents may start needing our help, as Mindy's 89-year-old father did when her mother was on the respirator. We usually enter middle age with both parents alive. We often leave that stage having lost at least one of them. Some of us start to wonder about the "is that all there is'ness" of life. No wonder we're at the bottom of the well-being curve. But wait, that isn't the whole story. Not at all.

Remember, middle age is also the time when that curve starts going back up. Research from the MIDUS studies may shed some light on why. While midlife is a time of multiple challenges, it's also a time of developing a sense of mastery over those challenges and an opportunity for more character strengths to emerge or grow. When psychologists

David Almeida and Melanie Horn asked people of all ages about their stress levels, they found the most stress in those under the age of 59. But they also found that those between the ages of 40 and 59 felt the most *in control of* those stresses. As one 58-year-old woman told us, "I'm still very stressed, but I handle it better." While we're learning about all that's not in our control—we can't force our teenagers to drive under the speed limit when we're not with them, for instance—we're learning from our mistakes and yet providing guidance just the same.

## OLDER AGE

Even though many youth regard old age as a foreign country, in the words of author May Sarton, youth and old age are often mirror images of each other. Just as Madeline has her whole life to look forward to, her grandmother, Jimmie, has a long past to look back on. Both share a similar weightlessness compared with middle-agers: no children to take care of day to day, not yet (or no longer) taking care of parents. Whereas the young wonder what will happen down the road, the elder knows exactly what happened down the road. With one exception.

Just as young adults might wonder what they'll be doing with the rest of their lives, older adults wonder about their health and how long they will be able to maintain their independence, which is so precious to them. On this front, much of the news is positive for elders, as we're living longer, healthier lives than at any time in the past.

Erik Erikson noted that the primary task of our later years is to make peace with our lives. Laura Carstensen, founding director of the Stanford Center on Longevity, agrees. Her socioemotional selectivity theory suggests that as we age and have a lot less time ahead of us than behind us, we learn to live in the present moment, focus on the bigger picture, and better prioritize and appreciate our lives and our relationships with other people. Thus, we gather and develop our character strengths—growing new and bigger branches on the oak tree—through years of coping with life's negatives and appreciating life's positives, learning to enjoy the good parts and make the best of the bad ones. As William May suggests, many older adults have learned to *travel light*.

### Kate, Retired 75-year-old Psychiatrist; and Les Paul

Kate: "Overall, life feels more straightforward. You just live it. . . . You know that the road ahead is much shorter, and you have certain limitations you never had before, so there aren't that many roads now, and you know that what roads there are, you're just going to walk. And if you don't waste a whole lot of time being miserable about it, you just walk and enjoy it, or at least whatever is enjoyable about it."

Famed musician and guitar maker Les Paul was still playing in jazz clubs at age 93 when he told Matthew Orr of the *New York Times*: "When you're my age, you know that the end is in sight. How do you handle it? You live for the moment. The past is gone, and the future isn't here yet, and you ain't gonna change it no matter what you think." Or, as Helen, 91, once told the Aging and Illness Group, "I've made my will and I am ready to die, but I sure would like to see the new slipcovers on the furniture I ordered last week, before I go." (By the way, it's been a few years since she got her slipcovers, and Helen hasn't gone anywhere yet.)

This simplicity, or *traveling light*, may come about as a function of the older person's growing wisdom about how life works. Studies of wisdom suggest elders tend to have greater awareness, appreciation, and knowledge of the world; they know better which social and emotional goals to pursue; and they are more adept at managing relationships (Park et al., 2002; Carstensen, 2006; Luong et al., 2011). This only makes sense. As novelist Margaret Atwood once said, "Good judgment comes from experience. But experience comes from *bad* judgment" (italics ours). Elders have had a lot more years to make mistakes and a lot more chances to learn from them.

Austrian psychiatrist Viktor Frankl put it this way in his book *Man's Search for Meaning*.

> *The pessimist resembles a man who observes with fear and sadness that his wall calendar, from which he daily tears a sheet, grows thinner with each passing day. . . .*
>
> *On the other hand, the person who attacks the problems of life actively is like a man who removes each successive leaf from his calendar and files it neatly and carefully away with its predecessors, after first having jotted down a few diary notes on the back.*
>
> *He can reflect with pride and joy on all the richness set down in these notes, on all the life he has already lived to the fullest. What will it matter to him if he notices that he is growing old? Has he any reason to envy the young people whom he sees, or wax nostalgic over his own lost youth? What reasons has he to envy a young person? For*

*the possibilities that a young person has, the future which is in store for him?*

*"No, thank you," he will think. "Instead of possibilities, I have realities in my past, not only the reality of work done and of love loved, but of sufferings bravely suffered."* (124–125)

And so, an elder may continue to be generative, in Erikson's sense, to keep influencing and guiding the younger generations (if they'll allow it!) and to be a "keeper of the meaning," in Vaillant's sense, as a bridge to the past while still *traveling light* and feeling free to say what he or she thinks.

Perhaps that U-bend is starting to make sense, after all.

We'll talk more about ageism in future chapters, but it's useful to keep in mind why it's a subject that's not for elders only. There is a cascade of fears across the years from young to middle and older age that colors our views of both elders and the very idea of aging. These fears affect us at any age. We're so good at noticing all the things that seem to go wrong as we get older that we might fail to notice those aspects that can be inspiring, even beautiful. Let's look at the character strengths and virtues in more detail in order to help us stop this domino effect of fear, so we of all ages can enjoy the present moment that much more.

## REFERENCES

Almeida, D., and Horn, M. (2004). Is daily life more stressful during middle adulthood? In O. G. Brim, C. D. Ryff, and R. C. Kessler (eds.), *How Healthy Are We?: A National Study of Well-Being at Midlife* (pp. 425–451). Chicago: University of Chicago Press.

Atwood, M. (2009, September/October 2009). The pressure to be wise. *AARP Magazine*, 28–29.

Carstensen, L. L. (2006). The influence of a sense of time on human development. *Science*, *312*(5782), 1913–1915.

Carstensen, L. L., Pasupathi, M., Mayr, U., and Nesselroade, J. R. (2000). Emotional experience in everyday life across the adult life span. *J Pers Soc Psychol*, *79*(4), 644–655.

Erikson, E. H. (1950). *Childhood and Society*. New York: Norton.

Erikson, E. H. (1959). *Identity and the Life Cycle*. New York: Norton.

Frankl, V. E. (1963). *Man's Search for Meaning: An Introduction to Logotherapy*. Boston: Beacon Press.

Luong, G., Charles, S. T., and Fingerman, K. L. (2011). Better with age: Social relationships across adulthood. *J Soc Pers Relat*, *28*(1), 9–23.

May, W. (1986). The virtues and vices of the elderly. In T. R. Cole and S. A. Gadow (eds.), *What Does It Mean to Grow Old: Reflections from the Humanities*. Durham, NC: Duke University Press.

Orr, M. (2009, August 13, 2009). Last word: Les Paul. *The New York Times*. Retrieved from http://www.nytimes.com/video/obituaries/1247463983106/last-word-les-paul.html

Park, D. C., Lautenschlager, G., Hedden, T., Davidson, N. S., Smith, A. D., and Smith, P. K. (2002). Models of visuospatial and verbal memory across the adult life span. *Psychol Aging*, *17*(2), 299–320.

Peterson, C., and Seligman, M. E. P. (2004). *Character Strengths and Virtues: A Handbook and Classification*. New York: Oxford University Press.

Sarton, M. (1973). *As We Are Now*. New York: W.W. Norton.

Stengel, R. (2009). *Mandela's Way*. New York: Crown Archetype.

Vaillant, G. E. (1993). *The Wisdom of the Ego*. Cambridge, Mass.: Harvard University Press.

# 3

# Character Strengths and Virtues

Confucius believed that proper character took time to develop. Similarly, William May suggests that we are both the "authors and coauthors" of our lives: our stories unfold over time and in the context of our experiences and our roles in the world with other people.

When we speak of character, we are referring to attitudes that people might be born with or ones they have cultivated—or may yet learn to cultivate—over time, as they've learned the best ways to cope with stressful situations. Character strengths are those aspects of character that are particularly helpful in this endeavor and, even more generally, those aspects of character that help us to feel like we are living meaningful lives.

Anthropologist Sharon Kaufman suggests that we develop an ageless self, or a core identity, despite the many changing events that unfold over the course of a long life. She notes that as we live, we develop a story of our lives that is compatible with how we see ourselves—recalling the character strengths that have provided the framework for a life lived, despite our mistakes and, sometimes, because of what we learned from those mistakes. Our character—or ageless self—and our character strengths integrate the past with the present, providing a sense of continuity and comfort.

## THE EXTRAORDINARY PERSON IN EXTRAORDINARY CIRCUMSTANCES

The case of Nelson Mandela provides a wonderful example of this sense of continuity, in the guise of a poem, which he kept in his pocket throughout his twenty-seven years of incarceration in South Africa's most notorious prisons. When those twenty-seven years started, he was a revolutionary fighting the Apartheid government of South Africa. When they ended, he was a leader fighting to keep post-Apartheid South Africa together. Mandela the fighter was transformed over time into Mandela the peacemaker (Stengel 2009, Carlin 2008).

While Mandela credits aspects of his imprisonment for that transformation, he credits something else for his fortitude and ability to maintain his sense of self, a poem he reread every day. It invigorated him for his struggle to maintain his dignity in deplorable conditions and to fight for the nation he wanted his country to become. But it was no accident that he'd chosen that poem to begin with. He chose it because it matched up with some aspect of his character—his ageless self—that gave him strength and that he wished to cultivate further.

The poem was "Invictus," composed by William Ernest Henley in 1875 while he was recuperating after the loss of his leg to tubercular arthritis.

"Invictus"
Out of the night that covers me,
Black as the pit from pole to pole,
I thank whatever gods may be
For my unconquerable soul.

In the fell clutch of circumstance
I have not winced nor cried aloud.
Under the bludgeonings of chance
My head is bloody, but unbowed.

Beyond this place of wrath and tears
Looms but the Horror of the shade,
And yet the menace of the years
Finds and shall find me unafraid.

It matters not how strait the gate,
How charged with punishments the scroll,
I am the master of my fate
I am the captain of my soul.

We can see in this poem the seeds of the future elder statesman who would come to believe in discipline and self-control—in being the master of his fate and the captain of his soul. What drew Mandela to this poem suggests something about his character. But it was his evolution over time in response to his dire circumstances that allowed his true character and character strengths to fully form and manifest themselves, both privately and publically.

It is not an accident that Mandela was in his 70s when he ushered in the peaceful post-Apartheid era and walked into a rugby stadium with thousands of South Africans, black and white, screaming together in delight, "NELSON! NELSON!" Our character doesn't unfold overnight. It takes time to mature, and it takes time for other people to learn who we are and respond.

## CHARACTER STRENGTHS IN
## EVERYDAY LIFE

This unfolding of character doesn't happen only for extraordinary people, it happens for the rest of us, too. We all have to deal with life's random moments of mercilessness—illnesses, betrayals, crises of faith—and we all mature over time. The interaction of continuity and development over time is vital to our sense of ourselves as whole and as leading meaningful lives. For instance, nonagenarian Helen, whom we mentioned earlier, once told us, "I came out of my shell at 70!" Rather than having changed into some other person she'd never met before, she experienced herself as one continuous person who'd managed to grow and develop even at what others would consider an old age. (Now in her 90s, she isn't certain that she would still consider 70 all that old.)

When looking at the accomplishments of an extraordinary person like Nelson Mandela, it is easy to assume that the term *character strength* refers to some kind of superhuman quality that helps some special people thrive in the face of extraordinary circumstances. In fact, it's a term that is also relevant to how ordinary people live ordinary lives, what we learn from our experiences over time, and how we thrive personally, as a community, and as a species.

Over the centuries, many writers, philosophers, and religious leaders have explored the question of the best way to live, and they have come up with guidelines for living our best lives. These guidelines are often referred to as *virtues*. Even a casual glance would indicate a good deal of overlap between different conceptualizations. For example, the Greeks spoke of the four virtues of temperance, prudence, courage, and justice. Benjamin Franklin wrote of thirteen virtues, including temperance, justice, sincerity, and tranquility, among others. The Buddhist tradition of harmony in the self and in the community speaks to similar qualities. Years later, Mandela included in his lessons for life such guidelines as be measured, see the good in others, and have a core principle (Stengel, 2009).

Over the past twenty years, there has been a movement in psychology to study people's positive traits and how they can be harnessed to improve their sense of well-being. Of particular interest to us is a remarkable effort by a panel of psychologists to study the world's traditional religions and philosophies, in a sense, pooling all their resources with our resources.

Over the course of three years, this panel produced a list of core virtues gleaned from the major philosophies and religions. They examined the virtues and character strengths that all groups appeared to have in common; in other words, they wanted to know which character strengths, or virtues, appeared across time and culture. Christopher Peterson and Martin Seligman published the list in 2004. The panel found that there were many similarities in the positive qualities identified, whether they were described in secular or religious texts, and irrespective of Eastern or Western cultures, or ancient or modern peoples.

The group found twenty-four character strengths, which they grouped into six categories, or virtues, that were present across the diverse cultures and across the centuries: wisdom, courage, humanity, justice, temperance, and transcendence. They suggest that these traits may have been selected and maintained in order to meet specific survival needs: "Without biologically predisposed mechanisms that allowed our ancestors to generate, recognize, and celebrate corrective virtues, their social groups would have died out quickly. The ubiquitous virtues, we believe, are what allow the human animal to struggle against and to triumph over what is darkest within us" (52).

Sometimes, survival is simply a matter of luck. But, other times, it is a matter of cultivating those qualities that best help us survive.

## AGE, THE VIRTUES, AND THE ISSUE OF CONTROL

When one explores these virtues in more detail, it becomes clear how they often come to be associated with elders.

William May suggests that "virtues grow only through res-
olution, struggle, perhaps prayer, and perseverance" (50), all
of which are more likely to play out over the long haul. In
a beautiful essay about falling in love in her 70s, writer Eve
Pell describes it this way:

> *Old love is different. In our 70s and 80s, we had been*
> *through enough of life's ups and downs to know who we*
> *were, and we had learned to compromise. We knew some-*
> *thing about death because we had seen loved ones die. The*
> *finish line was drawing closer. Why not have one last blos-*
> *soming of the heart?*
>
> *I was no longer so pretty, but I was not so neurotic*
> *either. I had survived loss and mistakes and ill-considered*
> *decisions; if this relationship failed, I'd survive that too.*
> (ST6)

In older age, we become less reactive, less overinvested in
success. We know well how things don't always go our way
and that there is a limit to what we can control. It's because
of that hard-won knowledge that Eve Pell can say, if this
relationship fails, she'll survive that, too. But she won't let
fear of what might happen in the future keep her from
enjoying the relationship in front of her. She cannot control
what will happen in the relationship—or even know what
will happen—but she can enjoy it in the meantime.

Often, what character strength comes down to is the
issue of control: using it wisely and recognizing when we
don't have it. Mandela looked back on his almost three
decades of imprisonment as the time when he learned
what he considered to be one of the most important character strengths: self-control. "The one thing you could control—that you *had* to control—was yourself. There was no

room for outbursts or self-indulgence or lack of discipline" (Stengel, 15). But the issue of control comes up even without such dire circumstances.

From childhood through early adulthood, we are usually gaining in our sense of control. Our visual motor coordination improves as we grow stronger; our knowledge of the world improves through schooling; and, with practice, we become more skilled at many areas of life. Once we hit adulthood, that trajectory starts to shift a bit. We can't always get the jobs we want, or the promotions; we may not have as much free time to practice hobbies; we can't always console crying babies. The world starts reminding us that there are many things we can't influence at will. The ultimate lesson in the limits of our control, of course, is the recognition of our mortality. Try as we might over the millennia, we still don't get to be immortal.

But that doesn't mean we have zero control, of course. For instance, we may still die, but we tend to die a lot later than we used to. And we may not always be able to console crying babies, but often, we figure it out over time. Both older age and adversity ensure we learn not only our limitations but also our strengths. And they often have the habit of providing the context in which we learn who and what make our lives worth living.

As May points out, not all elders are virtuous, and virtues certainly develop when we're younger. But one thing elders are—survivors of life. And, like Eve Pell, we've had a longer incubation period when it comes to learning about how life works and how to cultivate our own sense of happiness and well-being. Character strengths and virtues grow out of life crises and, at the same time, they help sustain us through them. Jimmie is and continues to be one such survivor, and Mindy, a two-time breast cancer patient, hopes to continue to be another such survivor for a long time.

The virtues and character strengths we'll explore in detail are:

- *Transcendence*
- *Humor*
- *Humanity and social justice*
- *Courage*
- *Wisdom*
- *Temperance*
- *Passing on wisdom to the young*
- *Appreciating the cycle of life, including its end*

## THE VIRTUES AND THE RISE OF THE VINTAGE READERS BOOK CLUB

As we described in the Introduction, one way we have been exploring virtues and character strengths is through the readings and discussions of the Vintage Readers Book Club. The name has a double meaning, because we initially set out to read the Harvard Classics, of which there are about fifty. Never say we are shying away from a lengthy task that might be seen by some as likely to outlast our days. It has been an exciting and intergenerational discussion as well as a way to encourage intellectual activity for elders who might otherwise be isolated at home and having trouble motivating themselves to read on their own.

The Vintage group is now drawing people in their 60s through their 90s (plus some staff members in their 30s to 50s, as well). One of the most fascinating aspects of this group of elders is that the subject of age rarely, if ever, comes up. It is the subject of life in general that interests them.

The group's first discussion was based on the *Autobiography of Benjamin Franklin*, written when he was in his 70s. His descriptions are fresh and appealing, even today, in what is thought to be the first-ever American self-help program, predating modern-day Dale Carnegie's famous program or more modern examples, such as the Happiness Project. As Franklin writes, "I conceived the bold and arduous project of arriving at moral perfection. . .. As I knew, or thought I knew, what was right and wrong, I did not see why I might not *always* do the one and avoid the other." To that end, he created a diary with one page per virtue, with each page divided into seven for each day of the week. He recorded failures in each virtue category by putting a little black spot in the proper column.

Franklin's goal was to have as few black marks as possible as the year progressed. His list of thirteen virtues was based on his readings. He started with temperance in an effort to control his behavior, adding justice, tranquility, and sincerity along the way. He ultimately added humility, though he joked that, "Even if I could conceive that I have completely overcome it, I should probably be proud of my humility." After years of painstakingly recording his virtues and faults, Franklin ultimately gave up, noting that not only was attaining perfection unlikely, even if it were possible, the alleged achievement of perfection would annoy others. (For a complete list of the Vintage Readers Book Club titles, see the appendix.)

Before we explore in detail the virtues and character strengths, it's worth taking a look back in time. Because the virtues are not the only subject people have been grappling with over the millennia. It might come as a surprise to many people to learn that aging—even in very advanced years—is not an issue only for modern times. People have been doing it, thinking about it, and grappling with it for a very long time.

## REFERENCES

Carlin, J. (2008). *Playing the Enemy: Nelson Mandela and the Game That Made a Nation.* New York: Penguin Press.

Franklin, B. (1961). *The Autobiography and Other Writings.* New York: Penguin.

Kaufman, S. R. (1986). *The Ageless Self: Sources and Meaning in Late Life.* Madison: University of Wiconsin Press.

May, W. (1986). The virtues and vices of the elderly. In T. R. Cole and S. A. Gadow (eds.), *What Does It Mean to Grow Old: Reflections from the Humanities.* Durham, NC: Duke University Press.

Pell, E. (2013, January 27, 2013). The race grows sweeter near its final lap. *New York Times*, p. ST6.

Peterson, C., and Seligman, M. E. P. (2004). *Character Strengths and Virtues: A Handbook and Classification.* New York: Oxford University Press.

Rubin, G. (2009). *The Happiness Project: Or, Why I Spent a Year Trying to Sing in the Morning, Clean My Closets, Fight Right, Read Aristotle, and Generally Have More Fun.* New York: Harper.

Stengel, R. (2009). *Mandela's Way.* New York: Crown Archetype.

# 4

# Older Age in the Olden Days

## A Brief History of Aging in the Western World

*Aging is a moral and spiritual frontier because its unknowns, terrors, and mysteries cannot be successfully crossed without humility and self-knowledge, without love and compassion, without acceptance of physical decline and mortality, and a sense of the sacred.*

—Thomas R. Cole, *The Journey of Life*

## ASSUMPTIONS ABOUT AGING AND THE STORY OF MR. S

Mr. S, a writer in his 90s, was asked to appear in court. His sons believed he was no longer competent to handle his estate. Mr. S spoke in his own defense. He agreed that he might have neglected his work recently because he had been finishing a play. After he read his play to the court, the case was quickly dismissed.

Does this sound like a story you might have read about in the newspaper recently?

It so happens that Mr. S was Sophocles, and the play was his masterpiece, *Oedipus in Colonus*, according to Cicero in his *Essay on Old Age*, written in 44 BC (and a Vintage Readers Book Club title).

It's commonly assumed that in the old days, old age was valued and respected, even venerated, and that the modern era brought with it a decline in respect for older age.

But historians have challenged this assumption and have marshaled a great deal of evidence to combat the common myths about the history of aging and older age.

Another commonly held belief is that old age is, itself, a modern phenomenon, thanks to modern medicine. And there is some truth to that. In ancient Greece, the life expectancy at birth was only 20 to 30. By 1900, it was only up to around 50 compared with around 80, which is what it is now. In fact, though, there are many examples of men and women throughout recorded history who lived well into their 80s and 90s. The low life expectancy in olden times was due to very high infant mortality. Before the twentieth century, elders couldn't be sure that younger people would outlive them. For many centuries, death was associated at least as much with childhood as with old age.

Getting a picture of old age throughout history—both how it was thought of and how it was actually experienced in people's day-to-day lives—is complicated. There were no social scientists recording data, and when age was written about, it was rarely written by the aged themselves. Further, not all writings survived long enough for historians to find them. For example, many people have heard of the labors of Hercules in Greek myth but few are familiar with his battle against *Geras*, the personification of old age, which is depicted only on pottery. The actual story is lost. Also, the experiences of women, the poor, and servants are rarely mentioned before the seventeenth or eighteenth centuries.

Another difficulty in thinking about the history of aging is that we're all aging all the time; as long as we're alive, we're aging. Historically, older age has been thought to start anywhere from age 35 to age 70. Regardless of when we think older age starts, it lasts for decades, making for a very heterogeneous group. Further, some people object to thinking in terms of age groups at all. As one 65-year-old Englishwoman complained to researchers, "it's this habit of wanting to treat all people of a certain age group in the same way that seems wrong, whatever that age group is. People are no longer allowed to be individuals." One look around shows she has a point. Not all 65-year-olds experience being 65 the same way. Some are barely even aware of their age. One popular quote has it that old age is 10 years older than I am.

Yet another complication is the question of positivity versus negativity. As we'll see, sometimes attitudes about aging were very harsh; other times, they were seemingly positive. And yet, in practice, elders might be treated far better in the harsher times than in the "positive" ones.

Despite these challenges, historians have managed to piece together glimpses into attitudes toward aging through the millennia. What we know historically has been enriched by also looking at the way it was depicted in art and writings. Some issues come up again and again, even into our time. In one way or another, aging has been associated with questions of health and independence and fears of poverty and stigma in every era, including our own. Even the wealthy often had reason to fear becoming poor in older age. One affluent writer recently described this anxiety in *The New York Times Magazine*: "There but for the grace of a Chanel jacket go I. . . . This is true of so many women I know . . . ending up a bag lady is our darkest and clammiest fear" (Schwarzbaum 2013, 58). Religion has also played a particularly important role in the perception of aging throughout much of history, though it has had different effects in different countries and at different times.

Generally, we see some patterns developing over time. For one, as life expectancy got longer, society became more secularized, and images of the afterlife had less of an effect on day-to-day life. In the Middle Ages, aging was associated with Judgment Day and salvation, later becoming associated in people's minds with health and success as measures of morality, and, finally, with a focus on health and financial security in and of themselves.

Historian Thomas Cole (1992) points out that, over time, a new way of looking at aging started to take hold, and life was viewed in a more unified way. Rather than just a preprogrammed unfolding of a biologically and socially structured process, aging started to be viewed as a personal journey, taking into account people's individual spiritual and emotional experiences of aging.

Also, early thinkers tended to view age in terms of different kinds of staging systems, often using natural phenomena as metaphors for times of life. Some divided life into three stages, relating each to a different time of day, nighttime being the last stage. Others thought life unfolded in four stages, like the seasons, with winter standing in for our later years. Still others espoused a seven-stage system, and others, ten stages.

Whether viewing life in terms of stages or as a journey, one theme unites us all across different ages and different eras: the questions of what we can control in life, what we can't, and what makes our lives meaningful in the first place.

## ANTIQUITY: THE GRECO-ROMAN ERA

Aristotle divided life into three stages: growth, stasis, and decline. He believed middle age was the prime of life, when we are free of the negative traits of youth and older age. The young, he felt, were changeable, while he attributed to the old a host of unpleasant descriptions—small-minded, suspicious, malicious, and unfazed by what other people think. It's an interesting comment on the times that the members of the Vintage Readers Book Club think this last trait is actually one of the *benefits* of older age. Another "negative" ascribed to older people was that they loved life to excess! Sophocles suggested that "no one loves life like an ageing man" (Parkin 2005, 305). In modern times, we think of loving life as a good thing. It would be a couple of millennia before anyone would ask how aging women felt, too.

Interestingly, the authoritarian Spartans had a somewhat better view of aging than other cultures of the time, including the democratic Athenians. Spartans spoke deferentially of old age and were governed by the *Geroussia*, or council of elders that consisted of men in their 60s.

But they were the exceptions. In general, ancient Greeks revered youth and beauty. Power and wealth were concentrated in the hands not of elders but of their children. The literature of the day was not kind to older age, peppered with descriptions like "'hateful', 'accursed', . . . 'sorrowful', . . . 'wearying, hated even by the Gods'" (Falkner and de Luce 1992, 6). Older women, when referred to at all, were often depicted as sex-crazed and drunk. While there were some characters in the literature who represented wisdom in older age, as in Homer's *Nestor*, there was no assumption that wisdom came with age.

For men, the notion of elderhood often coincided with the marriage of their sons (commonly around age 60 for the father). Fathers were then expected to transfer their businesses and estates to their sons who were deemed better equipped to handle them. With these transfers also went elders' sense of authority and security. For women, elderhood was more biologically determined, starting with menopause, when they lost their ability to reproduce. Children were expected to care for their elders in service of *threpteria*, or repayment of the debt of nurture. Sometimes, this was enforced as law. But, in general, this system reinforced elders' insecurity and dependence on others, especially as they couldn't be sure their children would survive long enough to care for them or that they would be treated well by their children.

The Romans had a more patriarchal system, with the patriarch remaining head of the household for life; he was known as the *paterfamilias*. Only the *paterfamilias* was legally considered an adult, even if his sons were 30 years old. While this might have made for more financial security in older age for the eldest sons, it also made for a different kind of intergenerational tension; the literature of the time describes how sons waited for their fathers to die so they could come into their own. The Romans also believed in the concept of *tempestivitas*, the idea that every age has its own appropriate code of behavior. But elders were more likely than younger people to be criticized for violating it. And Roman literature also has many rcfcrences to "hateful" old age.

With one notable exception, most physicians agreed with Aristotle's view of old age as a disease. His theory that its main cause was a loss of heat would hold sway for more than two millennia. As late as 1858, Oliver Wendell Holmes would write, "The human body is a furnace. . .. When the fire slackens, life declines" (1873/2013). Aristotle believed this loss of heat also damaged the soul.

Galen, the physician/philosopher, was the holdout who thought of aging as a natural process, and he held that old age began at 48 (though 60 was the more common boundary for other thinkers). In addition to the loss of heat, he further hypothesized that aging depleted the body of moisture as well and urged elders to keep their bodies warm and moist for maximum comfort. His recommendations included a light diet, gentle exercise, reading, and travel. Foods to stay away from included milk and many vegetables, while his idea of healthy foods included plums, for their laxative effects, as well as lean meat, human breast milk, and wine.

In general, the Greek physicians divided life into four stages—childhood, youth, maturity, and old age. It was unusual for families to include members of all stages for very long. Multigenerational families were rarely mentioned in the literature. It was unusual for adults to have living grandparents. By the age of 10, only half had any living grandparent at all. And yet some individuals lived long, productive lives. The famous playwright, Aeschylus, wrote the *Oresteia* at age 67, the poet Pindar continued to compose his odes up to his death at age 80, and Plato remained active until his death in his 80s.

The man who was often held up as the ideal of old age was Cato the Elder, who remained influential in the senate (originally from the Latin *senex*, meaning *old man*) until his death at age 85. In 44 BC, Cicero used Cato's reputation to refute what he considered his society's false beliefs about aging in his "Essay on Old Age." Writing the essay as if it was a dialogue between Cato and younger friends who want to understand what older age is like, Cicero tackled each myth (16). His arguments would become highly influential during both the Renaissance and Enlightenment eras. But even Cicero admitted that his view of aging might apply only to those with the resources to feel financially secure.

The first myth Cicero attacked was that older age "incapacitates a man for acting in the affairs of the world." On the contrary, he argued that the prudence of the older generation served as an important antidote to the "hotheaded" youth in the Forum.

The second belief was that old age "produces great infirmities of the body." Here, Cicero found some justification. Whether it's hearing, vision, speed, mobility, or a host of other possibilities, older age is for many—then as now—a time of diminishing physical abilities, though there is a fortunate group for whom this isn't true. His advice for maintaining health mirrored Galen's: controlled eating and drinking, and proper exercise for both mind and body.

The third myth was that old age "disqualifies him from the enjoyment of the sensual gratifications." In fact, the notion that older age was not a time for sexual gratification will remain a consistent theme throughout much of history. Even Cicero didn't argue with it. While he still found eating and drinking to be sensual pleasures, sex was less so. But, he countered, being less inclined sexually was adaptive. As he wrote, it is "sensual and intemperate youth [that] hands over a worn-out body to old age" in the first place.

The final myth was the fears associated with being "within the immediate verge of death." In fact, he found elders were far from preoccupied with death. Rather, they focused on living as fully as possible, accepting that nature "has appointed to the days of man, as to all things else, their proper limits" (83).

Cicero pointed out why it was in everyone's best interest for elders (at least the men; he didn't mention the women) to be as much a part of public life as the younger generation and that aging was not something to fear. His argument would last for many years, as the generations of the Renaissance and Enlightenment would rediscover his work and celebrate it. But despite the elegance of Cicero's defense of aging, historian Thomas Cole (1992) notes one unfortunate feature of his argument: he divided old age—and elders—into "good" and "bad," blaming negative aspects of aging on bad character: "I have known many. . . who never said a word of complaint against old age; for they were only too glad to be freed from the bondage of passion, and were not at all looked down upon by their friends. The fact is that the blame for all complaints of that kind is to be charged to character, not to a particular time of life" (Part I).

Having a hard time with infirmities due to aging was tantamount to not living one's life as one should. Cicero's argument can be very encouraging for younger people—I don't have to be afraid of aging, as long as I live in the right way and have the right attitude; I'm in control. But it can also have a negative effect on those who might be blamed if problems arise for having lived the wrong way. This leads to a larger question—is the very idea of looking at aging in a positive light a zero-sum game, where every attribute that's considered positive by one person will itself be necessarily harmful to another? The question of how to reconcile positive and negative aspects in a way that integrates theoretical ideas of aging and its actual day-to-day experience is an issue we struggle with to this day.

## THE MIDDLE AGES AND RENAISSANCE

By the fifth century, life expectancy in Europe had risen a bit, to around 40, with elders accounting for 5% to 8% of the population. These numbers would vary over the next millennium, as the plague was more likely to kill younger people than elders. At some points, the percentage of elders increased to 15%.

European society was agrarian and feudal; most people made their living working land that was owned by a central lord. Life was very tenuous. Violence, epidemics, and constant warfare were part of daily living. People were ready for death at any moment, regardless of age. In fact, men were more likely to die in battle than of old age. And that was the preferred way to go.

As Christianity became the dominant religion, its images of an afterlife helped create a sense of security. Even if life in this world was fragile, people could be comforted by life in the next world. Aging began to be viewed through a religious lens. In the earlier years, theology was the province of a learned elite who thought of aging as a reminder of original sin. Further, eternal life had a downside, depending on where you thought your soul would end up. Older age became associated in people's minds with judgment in the next world, as it was the last step before Judgment Day. Preachers used age as a metaphor for vice and sin, as opposed to youth, which symbolized the soul and salvation. They used images of decay in older age as a way to instill fear in younger people who were urged to tame their passions.

Not surprisingly, elders were not particularly valued in this system. While seventh century historian Isidore of Seville wrote of the wisdom of older age, he also described it as "wretched in terms of both the disabilities it inflicts and the loathing it incurs" (Parkin 2005, 31). Even in monasteries, elder monks weren't particularly valued and were sometimes sent back to their families. Damages for the wrongful death of an elder were less than those awarded in the cases of a younger adult and were similar to those for a child younger than 10.

One exception to this attitude was found in Venice, where the average age for leaders was 72. The Venetians believed age conferred wisdom and balance. This would also be true of some Renaissance cities during the later Middle Ages. Aging might also have been a more liberating experience for women than for men. Menopause was the boundary of old age for women who were sometimes offered public responsibilities as midwives and chaperones in their later years.

With limited resources to go around, elders were expected, as in antiquity, to retire from the world and transfer their land to their children. Peasant families experienced enormous tension over the question of when these transfers would take place. Sometimes, landlords forced aging farmers to give up their land, either to children or relatives. Sometimes, fathers were able to keep their status as head of the household and work the land together with their adult children. Retirement was often built into the child's marriage contract, with parents agreeing to transfer their farms by a certain age in return for promises of lifelong maintenance. How well the promises were kept, or enforced if they weren't kept, is unclear. For many elders, the situation was fraught with tension, both in terms of the fear of not being able to depend on their families to take care of them when needed and of their enforced dependence. Whether some also found their forced retirement a well-earned rest is unknown, but we can assume that depended on their social support system.

Financially, aging was harder on some groups than others, especially if they had no assets to live on. Teachers, for instance, had no job security and had to keep working into older age as long as they could. Artisans, like jewelers and furniture makers, on the other hand, were less likely to become obsolete and also might have pensions from their guilds to rely on. They might also have valuable assets to sell, if need be.

The late Middle Ages saw some important shifts. Merchants, bankers, and tradesmen became more successful, stimulating the economy. Society became more market oriented and urban, as the new middle class began to rise in the cities. Time, as a concept, was different for businessmen who needed more exact day-to-day measures than farmers did. The boundary of old age was now thought to be anywhere from 35 to 70, depending on the staging system. The average was around 40 or 50 or related to a turning point in the home, like the marriage of the youngest child. Men tended to live longer than women because of the dangers of childbirth and because women were more likely to tend to the sick, exposing themselves to more infection.

Elders were still expected to hand over their jobs and the management of their estates to the younger generation. In general, they were expected to give up worldly ambition and sexual passion and to atone, focus on good works, and prepare for death and salvation. Aging was depicted in a more ambivalent way than before. On the one hand, there were still many negative stereotypes. Older people were described as ignorant, cowardly, suspicious, and gloomy. Postmenopausal women, in particular, were seen as socially dangerous; menstrual blood was thought to be impure, and women's inability to get these "poisons" out of their bodies made them greedy and lecherous.

On the other hand, some positive images started to take hold, particularly in the writings of the poet Dante. While he agreed with the ancients that our intellectual and physical peaks were in middle age, he also believed our spiritual development continued throughout our lives, describing older age as a time of peace and spiritual elevation. Some positive stereotypes were that age brought wisdom, a greater sense of calm, less passion (which was seen as a positive at the time), and greater likelihood for atonement.

Like Cicero, some writers made a distinction between the "good" and "bad" elderly. In fact, one of the things that helped to bring about the Renaissance in the fourteenth century was a revival of interest in Cicero's work, after it was translated by the Italian poet Petrarch. In the late thirteenth century, Roger Bacon published *The Cure of Old Age and the Preservation of Youth*, and other prescriptive books on aging began to appear. Once again, positivity is in the eye of the beholder, as the ambiguity is made plain in Bacon's title itself. He described older age as a disease needing a cure; yet, he was optimistic that people had enough control to avoid it.

There were a number of different staging systems during this time—three, four, seven, and ten—depending on whether you were a physician, philosopher, biologist, or peasant (who might have learned it from songs). The most popular during the Renaissance was the seven ages of man, later immortalized in Jaques's "All the world's a stage" soliloquy in Shakespeare's *As You Like It*. While this depiction of older age is very negative—"second childishness and near oblivion"—so are Jaques's descriptions of all the earlier ages. There's a good reason he was known as "the melancholy Jaques."

By the late fifteenth century, the concept of time started to take on new overtones. Father Time was depicted as a figure with a scythe in one hand and an hourglass in the other. Time was wasting, and judgment was at hand. The invention of the printing press allowed ideas to be disseminated more rapidly. Cole (1992) suggests that a new notion was taking hold in addition to the idea of stages—that of the personal and spiritual journey toward God.

One image became particularly popular by the sixteenth century, that of the Ages of Life, or the Steps of Life. It showed life as a staircase, going from left to right. On each step sat a man of increasing age from left to right. For the first half of the staircase, each new step was higher than the one before. The highest stair was the one in the middle, with the strongest-looking man sitting on it, after which the steps descended, with each new step lower than the one before, and the man on each step looking more frail than the one before. To the right of the staircase, death waited. Frightening images of Judgment Day adorned the picture, with the words *memento mori*—remember death. The implication was clear. Old age was the prelude to death and judgment. Power (still) belonged to the middle aged. This image would remain popular in Europe for the next 350 years.

The sixteenth century would also see much bigger changes, as Martin Luther published his *95 Theses*, challenging the Catholic Church and sparking the Protestant Reformation and Counter-Reformation. These new ideas would have significant implications for how aging was viewed and how older people were treated. In addition, during this time of tremendous religious upheaval, the urban middle class kept growing, wanting stability, and nurturing a growing belief in individual self-control.

Spiritual issues were no longer only the province of the clergy. Ordinary people were discussing them, too. Fears of death and damnation became ever more vivid. Preachers not only warned of the approach of Judgment Day, they also described older age as a time of cowardice and vanity, which would make it harder to repent in later life. Older women were particularly associated with magic and death, leading to witch-hunts throughout the sixteenth and part of the seventeenth centuries. Religious texts stressed the challenge of death rather than of old age.

Despite this harsh portrait, some positive images of older age came through. Dutch and English paintings, for example, associated age with authority, and older congregants were seated up front in church in the most honored pews. Some religious groups, particularly Calvinist Protestants, saw old age itself as a kind of salvation; survival that long was proof of God's grace. When the first Europeans settled in America, it was this idea of aging that they brought with them, creating a very different image that would hold sway in the new colonies until a famous upstart rebellion would change things in the late 1700s.

## THE PURITAN ETHIC AND COLONIAL AMERICA

The early history of aging in America is a very positive one, despite the fact that the colonies were so young. According to historian David Hackett Fischer (1978), the median age was 16, even though the settlers in the northern colonies lived longer than their former neighbors in Europe (and longer than those in the southern colonies). Men who reached maturity and women who survived their child-bearing years could live to age 70. Some have said that New England "invented grandparents," as more family members survived long enough for grandchildren to know their grandparents.

Paradoxically, while the Puritan ethic may sound harsh to modern ears, it led to the veneration of aging in early America. Man was innately depraved and could not escape from suffering. It was his lot to accept his inherent sinfulness, physical decline, and disease and to find a way to come closer to God, despite, or even through, these losses. While suffering was inevitable, there was always hope for salvation through grace. Rather than a time to fear damnation, old age was considered a time for getting closer to God, as described in one of the most famous spiritual journeys of the time, John Bunyan's *Pilgrim's Progress*.

Wealth and power were also concentrated in the hands of elders. They owned the land, determined the amount and timing of inheritance for adult children, held the local offices, and dominated the powerful churches. Because there was enough land for fathers to give to their sons without having to give up their own, the earliest settlers had less intergenerational conflict. This would change as land became more scarce, at which time elders were again expected to transfer their worldly possessions and to focus instead on piety and faith.

Elders and the young had reciprocal obligations to each other. The young were expected to venerate the old, while the old were expected to treat the young with decency and understanding. It was generally agreed, "'grey heads' were wiser than 'green ones'" (Fischer 1978, 40). Unlike their

European counterparts, colonial American elders were expected to be useful, at least in ways deemed age appropriate. Those who found themselves destitute and without family to care for them were given community assistance but were expected to give whatever services they could. They were also obliged to be role models for the younger generation. The ideals of this period were stability, hierarchy, and community. At least, they were the ideals before the American Revolution.

## SEVENTEENTH AND EIGHTEENTH CENTURIES: THE ENLIGHTENMENT AND REVOLUTIONS (SCIENTIFIC AND OTHERWISE)

In Europe at the dawn of the seventeenth century, Shakespeare wrote his most famous—and most blistering—portrait of aging and the conflicts between aging parents and their children, *King Lear*. The shallow king couldn't tell the difference between true love and manipulation, giving up his kingdom to the wrong daughters who later turned on him. While Lear loses everything, his loyal nobleman, Gloucester, is also betrayed by his own illegitimate son and blinded as a result. He cries out mournfully, "as flies to wanton boys are we to the gods."

But images of older age started to change later in the century, as the educated classes became more secular and the scientific revolution began. The hysteria over witches subsided by mid-century. Older people began to be thought of as a group to be studied and understood. Mathematicians studied life expectancy, while philosopher Rene Descartes explored the aging process in his writings. Society became more affluent.

*King Lear* was now considered too grim. Seventy-five years after Shakespeare introduced it, Nahum Tate revised it for the stage, with a new, happy, ending. This optimistic version would become more popular than the original and was considered the definitive one for more than a century, before Shakespeare's original was reintroduced to the public in the nineteenth century.

While the apex of life was still considered to be middle age, more respectful portraits of older age began to be acknowledged. Alongside the old negative stereotypes were positive ones. Older men were considered more knowledgeable and better advisors than younger men, while older women were steadfast and devoted to their families.

This period of increasing affluence also saw more variability in aging and mortality. The wealthy were more likely both to live longer and to stay youthful looking longer. They were also more likely than their poorer counterparts to hold on to household power into old age. Ten percent of the population was over 60, and families included more living grandparents who could help with grandchildren if a parent fell ill or died. Northern European households were mostly nuclear, though three-generation households were more likely to be seen in Russia, the Baltics, and Spain.

Medicine hadn't changed much since the Middle Ages. Aging was still seen as an incurable disease involving loss of heat. Physicians' focus was on comfort and preventing premature aging. They prescribed diet (as before, foods that were warming and wet; this time, the suggestions were young meat, red wine, and milk, in small portions), exercise, staying in warm rooms, and avoiding negative emotions, like anxiety or anger.

Cicero enjoyed another revival in his popularity. In 1732, the Marquise de Lambert, an aristocratic French writer in her 60s, noted that his essay lacked advice for women. So, she wrote her own version, urging aging women to avoid passion and to retreat from social life. The Marquise apparently did not take her own advice about retiring; she organized one of the most important literary salons in Paris.

Life expectancy continued to rise in the early to mid-eighteenth century as society became more secular. At mid-century, in some parts of Europe, 42 percent of the population survived into their 60s or later. More attention began to be paid to *this* life, rather than the next. And, as in colonial America, old age began to be associated more with life than death. Rather than retiring, older adults were urged to stay independent as long as possible.

The image of old age began to be idealized and more sentimental. Memoirs and autobiographies included stories of grandparents, while aging writers explored the joys of older age, including grandparenting, which was becoming more common as more people lived longer. Aging writers also wrote about sex for the first time. Paintings still depicted scenes of physical deterioration in aging, such as blindness and missing teeth, but the images often retained a sense of dignity and appreciation for the accomplishments of a lifetime that elderhood also symbolized.

The French viewed elders in a particularly idealized way. When they revolted against King Louis XVI in the late 1780s, the revolutionaries sought elders' blessing, going so far as to create the Festival of Old Age to honor them. Exactly the opposite was happening on the other side of the

Atlantic Ocean. As a result of the American Revolution, old age was starting to lose its prestige.

## NINETEENTH CENTURY AND THE INDUSTRIAL REVOLUTION

One of the most popular American stories of the early nineteenth century was Washington Irving's *Rip Van Winkle*, published in 1819. Rip famously falls asleep on a mysterious mountain in the period just before the start of the American Revolution, and wakes up twenty years later to find the world has changed. King George III has been replaced by a new George, just as Rip himself has been replaced by his son, Rip Jr. After the town's initial confusion and resentment—Rip Sr. professes his loyalty to the king before he realizes he's on the wrong side of history and corrects himself—all is forgiven, and he is taken in by his daughter. Never one for work, he's happy to spend his days idly in her home. Unlike his earlier life, when his (now deceased) wife would complain about his lack of a work ethic—it was her nagging that he was trying to escape when he fell asleep in the first place—his cheery idleness is accepted.

The story beautifully illustrates the anxieties of growing older in a world where the rules had so drastically changed, while it reinforced the image of elders as useless and obsolete. Revolutionary America was opposed to all patriarchal authority, likening the king to a tyrannical father. Public officials were now forced to retire at age 60 or 70, and seating in church was determined by wealth, rather than age.

Economically, an even bigger shift was underway in both Europe and America, as the manufacturing industry grew and supplies of land became more limited. Transportation improved, as did the quality of goods. While the need for many skilled nonmanufacturing workers declined, some forms of work evolved into professions, like medicine and law.

By the first third of the nineteenth century, many men had left home to find work in towns and cities. The cities, and the new industries, were seen as young and vital, while the countryside was perceived as old and old-fashioned. The manufacturing economy increased the risk of poverty and disability in older adults who couldn't easily keep up the pace of technology or the requirements of the factories. Tensions between the generations grew, and old age started to be discussed officially as a social problem.

From a religious perspective, people saw God as a more benevolent and compassionate presence who would reward them for living correctly. They were less afraid of damnation. Ages of Life prints were more likely to include an image of the Garden of Eden than of Judgment Day. This generation believed that man could shape his own destiny through grit and hard work. They rejected the notion of limits, and their ideas of virtue revolved around independence and success. Health and long life were seen as moral issues, rewards for proper living that were under everyone's control. There was less focus on the spiritual life of elders and more on extending middle age and avoiding death as long as possible. And so, the image of older age was both idealized and feared at the same time. There was a great deal of advice for preparing for old age, but much less advice for the aged themselves. And there was little help for the aged poor, who were thought to have only themselves to blame for their plight. If they didn't have families that could, or wanted to, care for them, their only alternative was the poor house.

At the same time, the number of elders increased as life expectancy increased, especially by the middle of the century. This was largely thanks to the efforts of health reformers who demanded better water and sanitation, as well as medical advances, like acceptance of the germ theory of disease. Some reformers had an almost religious fervor about preaching physical perfectionism. Some claimed that with the right behavior (temperance, sexual restraint, vegetarianism, and exercise), people would be able to live healthfully for hundreds of years. While this was a secular version of aging, it still assigned moral weight to the experiences of older people, who could enjoy a long and healthy life if only they behaved well enough.

At that time, the medical view of aging remained fatalistic and assumed that the physical condition of older people could only deteriorate, not be made better. Doctors wouldn't revise the ancient Greek understanding of aging until the late nineteenth century, when they would start thinking more narrowly, and scientifically, in terms of how aging affected individual organs and the immune system, and how something might be done to help people with age-related problems.

By the end of the century, an interesting relationship started to develop between theoretical images of aging and the willingness to help aged people in need. Germany's Otto von Bismarck started the first organized pension plan in the 1880s. The rest of Europe quickly followed suit. The United States didn't offer one until 1935, after a contentious battle that equated help for elders with socialism, by which time more than 50% of elders had fallen beneath the poverty line.

At the same time, negative images of aging came back with fervor, not only acknowledging infirmities but exaggerating them, too. Paradoxically, positive images of aging led society to blame elders for their own problems and to refuse to help, while negative images did the opposite. This relationship didn't go unnoticed by twentieth century researchers and people in the helping professions who were fighting to get services and funds for older adults in need.

As pension plans became more popular, especially into the twentieth century, age once again was divided into three stages, similar to those described by Aristotle. This time, they were defined as the education years, the work years, and retirement. Cole points out that by the twentieth century, the journey of life had evolved from a focus on the afterlife, to a fervent belief in our ability to control our destiny in multiple areas of life, to the search for financial security and physical health. Aging was no longer related in people's minds to a spiritual journey. Security for the third stage of life meant different things to different people, as more people than ever before could look forward to a relaxed, financially secure future. However, others felt marginalized by this system because it kept them from feeling like they were leading useful and meaningful lives after a predetermined date.

## TWENTIETH CENTURY: THE DEMOCRATIZATION OF LONGEVITY

The greatest changes to our average lifespan occurred in the last 150 years, thanks to improved income, diet, public and private hygiene, and medicine. The survival curve was once shaped like a pyramid, with older age belonging to the smallest group and younger age belonging to the largest. By the end of the twentieth century, that pyramid became a rectangle—with as many in the older group as in the younger one. Some wonder if the future curve will be shaped more like a parachute, with more elders than middle-agers, young adults, or youngsters.

Aging now was seen less from a religious viewpoint and more from a medical and scientific one. Judgments about older age were based on productivity, and some of them were very harsh, even on the middle-agers. For example, William Osler, known as the father of modern medicine, reported in 1905 that a scientific assessment showed that men made most of their contributions to society before the age of 40 and almost all before age 50. He argued both for retirement and pensions in older age based on this study.

At around the same time, Elie Metchnikoff, the Nobel Prize–winning father of modern immunology, countered this view with his own belief—similar to that of Roger Bacon in the thirteenth century—that aging was a disease but one that could be treated. For Metchnikoff (1905, 1907), that meant fighting intestinal bacteria, which he thought caused the "disease" of aging. As in earlier times, he recommended sobriety, hygiene, and diet, and his food of choice was sour milk to fight the bacteria. As a result, a sour milk craze took hold for a while. Other theorists suggested even more outlandish possibilities such as extracts of animal sex glands for both men and women.

Dr. Ignatz Nascher broke with Metchnikoff and argued that aging was not a disease to be cured but, as Galen thought, a natural stage in life. It took years before this became the dominant view. Nascher coined the term *geriatrics* in 1909 (Thane, 2005), and geriatric medicine became a new medical field. Once again, Nascher felt that diet and exercise—both mental and physical—were the key to better aging. He also felt that medicine ignored older adults since it was assumed they wouldn't live much longer. Interestingly, medicine would enable us to get even older by mid-century, not through "cures" for older age but through treatments for diseases in people of all ages, such as heart disease, cancer, and hypertension, as well as the vaccines that were introduced earlier in life. In other words, what helped adults live longer and healthier lives were the same treatments that helped everyone else.

By the 1970s, Robert Butler had coined the term *ageism* to describe the many ways in which older adults were discriminated against by society and the negative stereotypes about them. As Cicero showed us, the term might have been new, but the concept was very old. However, one can argue that positive stereotypes are just as ageist as negative ones in that they treat older adults as if they were a monolithic group that's separate from everyone else who's younger. Positive stereotypes can lead to unfair expectations of all people of the same age. And some of us are still far less financially secure than others.

## RECONCILIATION

Rather than good versus bad character, twentieth century medicine ushered in the more sophisticated-sounding concepts of successful versus unsuccessful aging that we speak in terms of today. If you type "successful aging" into Google (to use a twenty-first century term), you will get more than 450,000 hits. But the old morality still creeps in. Is someone who's frail at age 80 an unsuccessful ager? Is aging only about keeping our bodies under as much control as possible?

As Cole (1992) argued, maybe we can find a more satisfying ideal of aging if we can get away from this kind of dualistic thinking and go back to the sense of life as a journey toward meaning. Whether that meaning comes from a religious source or a secular one, it's a pursuit that gives each individual life story a sense of integrity and wholeness. It's a given that there will be both positive experiences and negative ones along the way.

Throughout history, we have learned to control more and more of our environment and our bodies. But that control is never complete, regardless of our age. How we learn to accept that limitation is part of the journey and part of how we discover who we are and what's meaningful to us. Perhaps one of the most important lessons of history is the importance of learning to reconcile the good with the bad, the things we can control with the things we can't, the older with the younger. If we can do those things, we can better appreciate the full spectrum of the joys life can bring without fear of the future.

Maybe we can learn to go one better and begin to look forward to some aspects of that future.

## REFERENCES

Botelho, L. A. (2005). The 17th century. In P. Thane (ed.), *A History of Old Age* (pp. 113–174). New York: Oxford University Press.

Butler, R. N. (2008). *The Longevity Revolution: The Benefits and Challenges of Living a Long Life.* New York: Perseus.

Cicero, M. T. (1820). *An Essay on Old Age.* Translated by W. Melmoth. Google Ebook.

Cole, T. R. (1992). *The Journey of Life: A Cultural History of Aging in America* Cambridge: Cambridge University Press.

Cole, T. R. (2005). The 19th century. In P. Thane (ed.), *A History of Old Age* (pp. 211–262). New York: Oxford University Press.

Conrad, C. (1992). Old age in the modern and postmodern Western world. In T. R. Cole., D. D. van Tassel, and R. Kastenbaum (eds.), *Handbook of the Humanities and Aging* (pp. 62–95). New York: Springer.

Falkner, T. M. and de Luce, J. (1992). A view from antiquity: Greece, Rome, and elders. In T. R. Cole., D. D. van Tassel, and R. Kastenbaum (eds.), *Handbook of the Humanities and Aging* (pp. 3–39). New York: Springer.

Fischer, D. H. (1978). *Growing Old in America, Expanded Edition.* New York: Oxford University Press.

Holmes, O. W. (1873/2013). *The Autocrat of the Breakfast-Table.* Boston: James R. Osgood and Company/Project Gutenberg.

Irving, W. (1819). Rip Van Winkle: A posthumous writing of Diedrich Knickerbocker *Bartleby.com*. Retrieved from Bartleby. com website: http://www.bartleby.com/195/4.html

Metchnikoff, E. (1904). The Prolongation of Life, in T. R. Cole (1992). *The Journey of Life: A Cultural History of Aging in America*. Cambridge: Cambridge University Press.

Metchnikoff, E. (1907). A few remarks on soured milk, in T. R. Cole (1992). *The Journey of Life: A Cultural History of Aging in America.* Cambridge: Cambridge University Press.

Osler, W. (1905). The Fixed Period, in T. R. Cole (1992). *The Journey of Life: A Cultural History of Aging in America*. Cambridge: Cambridge University Press.

Parkin, T. G. (2005). The ancient Greek and Roman worlds. In P. Thane (ed.), *A History of Old Age* (pp. 31–70). New York: Oxford University Press.

Schwarzbaum, L. (2013, September 15, 2013). The fear that dare not speak its name. *The New York Times Sunday Magazine*, p. MM58.

Shahar, S. (2005). The Middle Ages and Renaissance. In P. Thane (ed.), *A History of Old Age* (pp. 71–112). London: Thames & Hudson Ltd.

Thane, P. (2005). The age of old age. In P. Thane (ed.), *A History of Old Age* (pp. 9–30). London: Thames & Hudson Ltd.

Thane, P. (2005). The 20th century. In P. Thane (ed.), *A History of Old Age* (pp. 263–300). London: Thames & Hudson Ltd.

Troyansky, D. G. (1992). The older person in the Western world: From the Middle Ages to the Industrial Revolution. In D. D. K. Cole.T.R.; van Tassel, R. (eds.), *Handbook of the Humanities and Aging* (pp. 40–61). New York: Springer.

Troyansky, D. G. (2005). The 18th century. In P. Thane (ed.), *A History of Old Age* (pp. 175–210). New York: Oxford University Press.

# Part II

# The Virtues

# 5

# The Virtue of Transcendence

## Beyond the Self

*I'm finding out as I'm aging that I am in love with the world. And I look right now, as we speak together, out my window in my studio, and I see my trees and my beautiful, beautiful maples that are hundreds of years old. . .*

—Maurice Sendak, 83, last interview, National Public Radio

*A few years ago, somebody asked me what time of my life did I like best. And I said, "Now."*

—Dr. Hedda Bolgar, psychoanalyst, at age 97

Transcendence, from the Latin word *transcendere* meaning to climb beyond, refers to the feeling of having a sense of meaning beyond ourselves. There are as many ways of experiencing transcendence as there are people. It can be a religious experience of feeling close to God; it can be a nonreligious but spiritual feeling of connectedness to other people, nature, or the universe; or it can refer to a secular experience of rising above a difficult situation. Ultimately, transcendence is related to a feeling of meaning and purpose in the world, a sense, even if only momentarily, of the joy of being alive.

Philosopher William May ties the need for transcendence to our mortality. "Death looms as an abyss," he suggests, "unless it can be set within the context of a transcendent meaning" (1986, 55). Psychiatrist Viktor Frankl (1963) relates transcendence to the "tragic triad" of human existence—pain, guilt, and death. Life is about so much more than these negatives, even if, sooner or later, we all have to deal with them. And it is often through the virtue of transcendence that we're able to remember that.

Transcendence can also refer to something very small. Every now and then, when Mindy drinks a cup of hot chocolate, she remembers the time when she was stuck outside in a blizzard, freezing, wet, and yearning for shelter. When she finally made it home, her husband, Rob, made her a cup of hot chocolate while she got into warm, dry clothes. Drinking the hot cocoa, she felt transported. It was because the world had felt so harsh only a moment before that she could appreciate the ways in which it could be beautiful, in the form of a loving partner and a hot drink.

We can experience transcendence at any age, but, as our colleague Kate reports, "I feel it more often and more comfortably now at 75. In older age, it is a quieter capacity for recognizing the treasures in existence." Maurice Sendak (2011), in his final radio interview with National Public Radio, explains why he is now so much better able to appreciate the beauty of his maples. He notes, "I can take time to see how beautiful they are. It is a blessing to get old. It is a blessing to find the time to do the things, to read the books, to listen to the music."

Psychoanalyst Hedda Bolgar was still seeing patients until shortly before her death at the age of 103. Many of them were in their 70s and 80s; to her, they were the younger generation. In an interview for the documentary *The Beauty of Aging*, she explained why she was at her happiest now, precisely because of her ability to transcend daily losses, and she related that ability to her age, "I don't know why people are so afraid of being old. It seems to me that what people see only is the loss or the deterioration or the minus, and they don't see that there are tremendous gains, the ease and the security of the feeling of essentially being able to cope" (Schur, 2013).

Dr. Bolgar, a World War II refugee, felt a sense of purpose because of her many profound experiences of suffering—war, famine, revolution—and that she was "put on this earth to accomplish certain things." This feeling of purposefulness helped her cope with and transcend her personal losses over the years, the most difficult being the death of her beloved husband when she was 65.

We see two kinds of transcendence at work in Professor Randy Pausch's famous *Last Lecture,* part of a Carnegie Mellon University lecture series about the wisdom you would try to impart to the world if you knew it was your last chance to teach. In Pausch's case, it really was his last chance, as he died of pancreatic cancer a few months later at age 47. The assignment gave him a new perspective on his life, as he thought about what he uniquely had to contribute to the world—the ability to help others achieve their dreams by telling them how he had achieved his own. As May might say, Pausch put his own unfair fate in the context of a transcendent experience. In her foreword to the book based on Pausch's lecture, his wife, Jai, describes how engaged he was in preparing this talk toward the end of his life and how meaningful it was (2008). He still saw himself as a lucky man, not only for fulfilling so many of his dreams but because of his wife and three children whom he loved dearly.

So, transcendence can come through something as small as a cup of cocoa or as large as an act of emotional survival, as immediate as a moment in time or as long lasting as a general attitude toward life.

*The Presence of Beauty: Transcendence as a Moment in Time*

*Imagine a music-lover sitting in the concert hall while the most noble measures of his favorite symphony resound in his ears. He feels that shiver of emotion which we experience in the presence of the purest beauty. Suppose now that at such a moment we should ask this person whether his life has meaning. He would have to reply that it had been worth while living if only to experience this ecstatic moment.*

—Viktor Frankl, *The Doctor and the Soul*, 43

Experiencing "the presence of the purest beauty" can transport us, taking us to another, far lovelier, place, even if all we're doing is sitting in a park. Our colleague Kate was particularly inspired by the story of a man she once met who'd been imprisoned by the Nazis and held in a tiny cell. He was cold, dirty, and terrified. The only ray of hope in his life came in the form of a tiny window at the top of his cell. All he could see, most of the time, was a sliver of sky. But every now and then, a bird would fly by. When he caught even the tiniest glimpse of it, he would suddenly be filled with hope. He found that bird—or the shadow he glimpsed—to be a thing of sublime beauty. It reminded him that somewhere the world was beautiful and that freedom still existed, if only for that bird. Seeing it fueled his dream that he would one day be just as free. The ugly world of his cell became a little less ugly and a place where hope could still bloom. One day he was freed and able to tell others his story of how a fleeting view of a bird had inspired him and kept his hope alive.

Dr. Frankl, another Nazi victim who survived Auschwitz, poignantly describes moments when he and his fellow inmates watched a beautiful sunset over the mountains of Salzburg while they were doing back-breaking labor in a rock quarry, always under the threat of being sent to the death camp section rather than the work detail. The men found great solace in the fact that whatever their individual fates, the beauty of nature, of which they were a part, would continue. They further seemed to find comfort in the very idea that their continued ability to appreciate moments of beauty transcended their dehumanized situation. Frankl credited such moments with the survival of his spirit, without which he believed he would surely have perished in the camps (though he does not dismiss the element of luck).

In their research on the partners of young men dying of AIDS in the 1980s, Crystal Park and Susan Folkman found that such moments of beauty were incredibly important in helping the healthy caregivers cope as they watched their partners slowly deteriorate and die. In the midst of the pain, watching a beautiful sunset together or admiring a particularly beautiful flower could bring them together in a shared special moment that transcended their heartbreaking situation. These moments made them feel a part of a greater, more beautiful world, different from the grim corner they experienced on a daily basis. Alongside many of their painful experiences, they were able to appreciate these positive experiences, which helped to revive their spirits. Often, the grieving surviving partners later looked back on these times with an almost reverent recall of their beauty.

Similarly, Hedda Bolgar loved to tend to the many flowers in her yard. "I have a very strong feeling of connection with everything that's alive," she says, including "animals, plants, trees, people" (Schur 2013). Benjamin Schechter, a physician in his 60s, similarly feels that his gardening transports him beyond the present moment, as does listening to Dvořák, Beethoven, Ella Fitzgerald, and Mel Tormé.

For Jimmie, it is sunrise, rather than sunset, that moves her. In the old days on the farm, the experience of hearing the chirping of the awakening birds and the cock-a-doodle-do of the roosters meant a new day was beginning. Though there aren't too many roosters around her home in New York City, she still feels like a part of nature when she hears the mourning doves cooing through her open window on summer mornings.

Beauty can come through nature, through art, music, or a piece of writing. A good book often transports us from our immediate contexts into the worlds we're reading about. An inspirational book can help us transcend difficult moments in our lives. Vintage Reader Eddie Weaver, an 88-year-old retired physicist, feels it when he reads poetry.

It isn't only reading that can transport us; the act of writing can do that, too. Sometimes, we use writing specifically to transcend difficult moments. Journaling has been found to help cancer survivors cope with their illness. The Memorial Sloan Kettering Cancer Center, for example, hosts a popular writing program known as Visible Ink. In one exercise, group members were asked to write a six-word memoir about the program. One woman wrote:

Bodies are fragile.

But words soar.

> *The Transcendent Nature of Love*
> *"Piglet sidled up to Pooh from behind.*
> *"Pooh?" he whispered.*
> *"Yes, Piglet?"*

*"Nothing," said Piglet, taking Pooh's hand.*

*"I just wanted to be sure of you."*

—A.A. Milne, *Winnie the Pooh*, 120

Mindy once asked the members of a cancer support group to share examples of times when they had felt most alive. These were their answers:

- *My memory of my four-year-old grandson running toward me with outstretched arms.*
- *My father tearing up at an award ceremony for my photography. The old man was not one to show emotions easily.*
- *Falling in love.*
- *Forging a new relationship with my mother after my father died of cancer.*
- *Saving a puppy with dysentery; now he's like my child.*
- *The day I married my wife while her mother was dying of cancer. It was intense.*

Notice how every answer is related to love. Not only romantic love but also of parents, even a pet.

For Frankl (1963, 1973), love transcends life itself. He describes a moment when he was on a forced march from his concentration camp on an icy, cold morning. Prisoners were whipped and rifle-butted by guards if they didn't move quickly enough. The threat of death was omnipresent. And Frankl suddenly thought of his wife. ". . . But my mind clung to my wife's image, imagining it with an uncanny acuteness. I heard her answering me, saw her smile, her frank and encouraging look. Real or not, her look was then more luminous than the sun which was beginning to rise. . . I understood how a man who has nothing left in this world still may know bliss."

Interestingly, Frankl confesses that at the time he didn't know whether his wife was even alive, and yet it didn't detract from how comforting her image was to him. "There was no need to know; nothing could touch the strength of my love, my thoughts, and the image of my beloved" (1963, 48–49).

Similarly, Randy Pausch confessed to the audience at the end of his lecture, "This talk's not for you, it's for my kids." As he describes in more detail in the book based on his lecture:

> *Under the ruse of giving an academic lecture, I was trying to put myself in a bottle that would one day wash up on the beach for my children. If I were a painter, I would have painted for them. If I were a musician, I would have composed music. But I am a lecturer. So I lectured. I lectured about the joy of life, about how much I appreciated life, even with so little of my own left. . . ..* (2008, xiv)

Relationships refer to a lot more than our family members. They refer to our relationships with friends, neighbors, and colleagues, too. Even pets. We've known many older people who find remarkable solace by having an animal to love. Mildred and Oscar Larch pour their love into their cockatiel, Jocko, who runs their household from his perch. Jocko wakes them every morning, demands his gourmet breakfast, chats with them during the day, and then is "put to bed" in the kind of nightly ritual often seen with children. Their love for their beloved pet runs deep, and they have been careful to make arrangements for his home if he outlives them. Laura Slutsky, a businesswoman in her 60s, feels her two dogs, Boo-boo and Shayna Punim, "are my life. They give me a purpose and a reason to come home."

### *The Broadening of Self: Transcendence and the Meaningful Life*

A meaningful life is made up of more than a string of transported moments with dead space in between. Another kind of transcendence comes through generally experiencing ourselves as part of something greater than ourselves. A religious person, for example, might feel like a part of God's plan. A nonreligious person may experience herself as a part of nature as a whole, as Bolgar describes.

Our causes, work, and creations help us feel like part of something larger than ourselves by giving us a responsibility to fulfill and a task on which to focus, instead of focusing on ourselves directly. The results of our projects may even outlive us, and others may appreciate our work long after we're gone. Like Pausch, each of us has unique contributions to make. Humorist Art Buchwald—who lived so much longer than expected that he was kicked out of hospice and sent home—felt his job was to use his talent for making people laugh, to help them be less afraid of death and dying. "Dying isn't hard," he said, "getting paid by Medicare is hard!" After leaving hospice, Buchwald revived his newspaper column and published his best-selling book, *Too Soon to Say Goodbye*.

Similarly, both of us felt we were part of something larger as we wrote this book about a subject that's relevant to everyone, sooner or later (whether we like it or not).

## Dorothy Kelly: Responsibilities to Others and Rising Above the Past

Dorothy Kelly grew up in the early twentieth century in a privileged home and a loving family. But she suffered from terrible shyness and severe anxiety to the point of suffering panic attacks in social situations, which made her even more shy. As was common at the time, Dorothy's symptoms went unrecognized and untreated. Her parents had great aspirations for her, but she opted out of college and took a job as a secretary in a publishing house. There, she met and married Bob, an ambitious editor who was fifteen years older and had little time for a young wife. They had two children in rapid succession, and the young mother found herself at home alone with them while her husband became very successful.

Dorothy began having panic attacks again. She became terrified that something bad was going to happen to her children or that she herself might die. One day when her head began to race and she couldn't catch her breath, she found that a drink of gin reduced the fear and made her feel better. Seeing a psychiatrist was out of the question because of the stigma. Ashamed, she remained a closet drinker until one day when her children were ages 6 and 4.

Bob came home from work to find Dorothy asleep while their children played by themselves. He immediately left her, taking their young children with him. While Dorothy got herself together enough to support herself with a secretarial job, she was crushed. She thought of suicide. Instead of acting on her thoughts, Dorothy attended Alcoholics Anonymous meetings at the suggestion of a friend from her office. Pursuing the twelve steps religiously, she not only recovered, she started helping other younger women with their drinking problems. She often felt that helping others helped her maintain her own sobriety, as well.

While Dorothy managed to have regular visits with her children during these years, they were limited. She was also acutely aware that she could not afford to buy them nice toys, and her modest apartment was a poor contrast to the large and beautifully furnished home in which they lived with their father and stepmother.

Dorothy continued her volunteer activity as she regained her life and married a compatible, loving man. She became a legend in the AA group. At her twenty-fifth anniversary of sobriety, twenty young women appeared to celebrate it and to thank her for her help. She had found a way to nurture younger women as a substitute for the mothering she was unable to give her own children. In her later years, she spoke with particular pride about the many young women she had sponsored and about the good feeling it gave her to see them doing well.

As her children matured, they came to understand Dorothy's problems and to show her their affection, sharing their own children with her. Dorothy's grandchildren became a source of great joy to her.

Like the transcendent moment, transcendent tasks can be very small and still have a large impact. In their classic study of elderly patients, Ellen Langer and Judith Rodin gave nursing home residents a plant to keep in their rooms. Half the residents had to care for the plant themselves, while nursing home staff tended to the plants in the rooms of the other half. The simple task of keeping the plants alive and watching them grow—of being responsible for and to them—led to a better quality of life for those who took care of their own plants. Remarkably, they had not only greater psychological well-being but better physical health, too.

Erik Erikson described how aging, in general, can lead to a broadening of the perspective of self in the context of a widening social radius. Older people often find great comfort in thinking beyond their finite selves. They become more concerned with the bigger problems of human justice, the quality of the environment, and what the next generations will have to face. They realize that they will not live to see this future. They begin to think beyond their self and the present to the future of their children, their protégés, and the planet. They become like the farmer Cicero described in his *Essay on Old Age* who takes joy in planting and cultivating young trees, even though he knows he won't live long enough to taste their fruit.

This change in thinking has been described by Dr. Lars Tornstam, a Swedish gerontologist, as gero-transcendence, the comforting sense of personal continuity with the larger universe that develops more in older age and enhances our experience of our lives. This is just like Hedda Bolgar's feeling of being connected to all living things. (See chapter 7 for more about this form of transcendence.)

*Laughing in the Chemo Room*

When Mindy was in treatment for stage II breast cancer in the fall of 2006, she and her husband, Rob, watched DVDs of the television sitcom *Arrested Development* while the IV was busily pumping poisonous chemicals into her arm. It was a show about the Bluth family, which first built its fortune on a frozen banana stand, and their highly dysfunctional relationships with each other. For example, here's a typical morning conversation between the matriarch and her adult son:

LUCILLE:  Get me a vodka rocks.

MICHAEL:  Mom, it's breakfast.

LUCILLE:  And a piece of toast.

Mindy and Rob laughed so hard that nurses found excuses to come in, craning their heads to see what could possibly be so funny that it beat out the realities of a chemo drip. Laughing at the horror of a mother from hell helped them laugh at the horror of their situation. Like Frankl's ability to appreciate the very fact that he could still appreciate a beautiful sunset, Mindy and Rob found that just knowing they could laugh was a relief in itself. The experience led Mindy to coin the term *chemo-worthy TV* for shows so good you can enjoy them even in the chemo room.

Humor is another important way that we transcend. It encourages us to rise above our troubles by helping us to look at our situation from a distance, and transports us to a nicer place. Being able to find and express humor is an important way of feeling our presence in the world and can also help us define ourselves. Art Buchwald became even more popular in his later years because of his ability to laugh at death and to help us do the same. Because humor is such an important part of the way we transcend our daily lives, we will try to understand all it accomplishes for us in chapter 6.

*Gratitude*

Another way we transcend is to be open to the experience of gratitude, either for other people or, simply, for the positive things in our lives. When Mindy had cancer, her gratitude for friends and family and what they did for her—driving four hours to take her children to the zoo, cooking dinner for her and her family, making a beautiful quilt for her to use during her treatment—was not merely a consolation prize for her suffering. It was actually a profoundly moving experience that gave her strength and reminded her that while the world might stink sometimes, it couldn't be all bad if it had such people in it.

Kate still remembers when she was hidden by Christian friends during the Holocaust and feels grateful to this day. "It's a feeling you carry with you the rest of your life," she says, "like wearing jewelry, only it's part of the jewelry in your head." She continues to visit her saviors who are still alive. Mindy's mother, also a Holocaust refugee, can remember the food and love offered to her and her family when they arrived at a refugee camp in Italy. She was too sick to eat any of the chocolates, eggs, and fruits lavished on her at the time, but a smile still springs to her lips whenever she remembers that day.

For older people, the limited time perspective also contributes to a sense of gratitude for having lived many years and even for life itself. Jimmie's husband, James, after a harrowing episode of illness, liked to joke that "not only am I glad to be here, I am glad to be anywhere."

## *Transcendence Through Memory*

Sometimes, just the memory of transcendent times is enough to make us feel better, like Frankl's load being lightened by the memory of his wife. As Jimmie's aged aunt once told her, "Be sure to start storing good memories, Jimmie. They help when you're old."

For this reason, Mindy waited in line for an hour and a half one unseasonably cold May day to get a frozen banana from the Bluth banana stand. It was a promotional gimmick heralding the release of new episodes of *Arrested Development*. Standing there brought back beautiful memories of a time when she was comforted by the laughter the show had inspired. A jaded New Yorker who doesn't usually fall for fads or gimmicks, Mindy, nonetheless, would do it again (even though the frozen banana tasted pretty awful). She keeps the blue wrapper above her computer to keep the memory alive.

Vintage Reader Lillian, 93, feels that digging up old memories feels very good, particularly when she can share them with someone else. Mental health counselor Tessie Hilton reports that her 80-something parents get great comfort from their memories, especially funny stories of their children's antics. Linda Moore's parents enjoy reminiscing with her, too. Her mother particularly loves telling stories about her own mother and to hear how much her mother meant, and continues to mean, to Linda.

## MEMORIES THAT SOOTHE AS THEY
## TRANSCEND

Sam is a courtly gentleman who, at age 95, has limited vision and mobility. He can't do many activities and spends a lot of time sitting in his room. But he describes how much he enjoys going over happy memories from earlier in his life, like his travels with his family to Europe and the Philippines. He especially likes thinking about one of the most meaningful periods of his life—his two years on a naval ship in the Pacific during World War II. Sam uses his memories of the past to substitute for the golf, tennis, and reading he would be doing if he were physically able.

Similarly, after he retired from his pediatric practice at age 88, Mindy's grandfather-in-law, Moe, enjoyed his daily activity of typing his memoir with his two index fingers. He particularly loved writing about his experience as a World War II Navy doctor on the USS *Crescent City*. Moe also enjoyed going over the many mementos he'd collected over the years, pictures from his days as the pediatrician for the Brooklyn Dodgers, thank-you notes from former patients who'd been inspired by him to go into medicine, and memories of particularly difficult or moving moments with patients. Sometimes, he would add his own notes on the backs of these photos and letters, reflecting, as Frankl once wrote, "with pride and joy on all the richness set down in these notes on all the life he had already lived to the fullest." (1963, 125) Now that Moe is gone, Mindy and Rob enjoy passing his stories on to his great-grandchildren.

*Open to It: The Transcendent Attitude*

Transcendence usually isn't something that just happens to a passive bystander. It helps to be receptive to the experience. We have to be willing to both stop *and* to smell the roses in order to appreciate and be affected by their beauty. As Kate says about the moments when she's particularly struck by a beautiful flower in the middle of an otherwise gray New York City sidewalk or the way the sun streams through the narrow, dreary streets at the right time of day, "I know it will happen again, because I'm open to it." And, the older she gets, the more open to it she finds herself: "It has come down to being quite comfortable finding it in smaller and smaller things, so that it's with me much more of the time." In this sense, it is more than an experience, it is an attitude toward life and what we expect from both it and ourselves. Jimmie's pleasure at hearing the morning birds singing was not something she was as aware of in her busy middle-age years.

Meaning isn't something that happens to us; it is something we impose on the world around us, making sense of it and finding a fulfilling place for ourselves in it. Linda Moore, for instance, is aware of coming "from a long line of intellectual depressives, so I make an effort to 'smell the flowers'." We have many avenues for experiencing a sense of meaning, whether by appreciating beautiful things, feeling part of the larger cosmos, or feeling responsible to others in that larger cosmos.

As in many other areas, aging can help us to accomplish these things, but aging alone is not enough. The more we've experienced transcendence, or a sense of meaning or purposefulness in our lives, the easier it is to be receptive to these experiences over time. Once we know how good it feels, we can appreciate how nice it is to find it where we can.

## Maureen Davis: Transcendence in Everyday Life

Maureen Davis is a prime example of someone who has always engaged life with zest and, at age 97, remains vibrant and busy every day. Her engagement with other people, compassion, and kindness show through the years. Maureen was Jimmie's teacher in the fifth, sixth, and seventh grades back home in rural Texas. It was her first teaching job; at age 20, she was barely older than her students. But Maureen dearly loved her work and the children. She taught with an enthusiasm and joy that endeared her to all her students and their parents. The kids recognized her affection, as she tried to be stern but could hardly suppress her laughter at their antics.

About ten years ago, when she was widowed, she chose to live in a nearby assisted living community to be sure that she didn't become a burden on anyone. She moved right in with her usual enthusiasm, commitment, and energy. "This is my new home," she declared, "and these people are my new family. I am going to enjoy it and help as much as I can."

And help she has: she teaches quilting classes, holds the weekly bingo games, mends residents' clothes, conducts the daily exercise class, and walks a half mile twice each day. A cheerful woman by nature, Maureen seeks out residents who seem lonely and cheers them up. Perhaps that's why the residents and staff have made her the Honorary Director. She experiences transcendence through her loving engagement with others and rarely speaks of the loss of her old world and way of life. Maureen is now as beloved by the people in her community as she had been by her students decades earlier.

## Transcendence and the Truth About Aging

Transcendence can be encouraged at any point in life; we can all benefit from the ability to learn from and move beyond the day-to-day details. Perhaps more than any other virtue, transcendence appears to be enhanced naturally by aging. As we age, we learn what we're grateful for in life, what makes us laugh, what moves us emotionally, and what we think is beautiful. The Vintage Readers Book Club members often transcend daily losses just by reading, discussing passages, and even arguing with each other about the ways the authors' ideas might apply to their own lives.

But one of the ways they most like to transcend is by making each other laugh. Singer Marilyn Maye—who is still selling out crowds at the age of 84—feels that a sense of humor is one of our most important assets for dealing with life, especially as we get older. "And if you don't have one," she advises, "latch onto someone who does!"

We agree that humor is such an important type of transcendence that it deserves its own chapter.

## REFERENCES

Buchwald, A. (2006). *Too Soon to Say Goodbye*. New York: Random House.

Erikson, E. H. (1959). *Identity and the Life Cycle*. New York: Norton.

Frankl, V. E. (1963). *Man's Search for Meaning: An Introduction to Logotherapy*. Boston: Beacon Press.

Frankl, V. E. (1973). *The Doctor and the Soul: From psychotherapy to Logotherapy*. New York: Vintage Books.

Hurwitz, M., Lilly, C., and Feldman, B. (writers) and P. Feig (director). (2005). Switch Hitter [Television], *Arrested Development*. Fox Broadcasting Company: 20th Century Fox.

Langer, E. J., and Rodin, J. (1976). The effects of choice and enhanced personal responsibility for the aged: a field experiment in an institutional setting. *J Pers Soc Psychol*, *34*(2), 191–198.

Lopez, S. (2013, May 15, 2013). She worked past age 100, inspired many more. *The Los Angeles Times*.

May, W. (1986). The virtues and vices of the elderly. In T. R. Cole and S. A. Gadow (eds.), *What Does It Mean to Grow Old: Reflections from the Humanities*. Durham, NC: Duke University Press.

Maye, M. (2013). [Personal communication].

Milne, A. A. (1956). *The House at Pooh Corner*. New York: E.P. Dutton & Co., Inc.

Park, C. and Folkman, S. (1997). Meaning in the context of stress and coping. *Review of General Psychology*, *1*(2), 115–144.

Pausch, R. and Zaslow, J. (2008). *The Last Lecture*. New York: Hyperion.

Schur, L. (Writer). (2013). Hedda. In L. M. Schur, L.T. (producer), *The Beauty of Aging*. web.

Sendak, M. (2011). On life, death, and children's lit. In T. Gross (ed.), *Fresh Air:* National Public Radio.

Tornstam, L. (1989). Gero-transcendence: A reformulation of the disengagement theory. *Aging (Milano)*, *1*(1), 55–63.

# 6

# The Underappreciated Virtue of Humor

## You Can't Spell *Joy* Without the *Oy*

*I plan to live forever. So far, so good.*
—Steven Wright

*When you're hungry, sing; when you're hurt, laugh.*
—Jewish saying

The members of the Vintage Readers Book Club agree that one of the most important things in life, after health, is our sense of humor. The "oy" mentioned in the subtitle refers to the Yiddish version of a lament, which means "Uh oh!," "Oh no!," and "Yikes!" all rolled into one. It's because of the oy's in life, that we appreciate and cultivate the joys. And one way we do that is through humor.

Vintage Reader Ellen, 62, feels humor reduces negative feelings such as aggressiveness and pain. Vintage Reader Phyllis, 78, thinks laughter "takes you out of yourself to a different plain. It's a long-lasting effect." Often, we make fun of what we fear in order to transcend it. A common fear among older people is what Jimmie calls "Alzheimerophobia," the fear of becoming demented. But even that subject raised a laugh from the group when Jimmie told entertainer Art Linkletter's story of visiting the Alzheimer's ward of a nursing home. "Do you know who I am?" he asked one elderly resident. "No," the woman kindly replied, "but if you go to the front desk, they'll tell you!" An elder couple joked that each of them had "half-heimers" and, together, they had "alls-heimer."

How does humor make us feel better?

## SOME HISTORY

The importance of humor goes back millennia. The face of Hilaritas, the Roman goddess of rejoicing and good humor, adorned Roman coins beginning with the Emperor Hadrian in the second century. The Romans considered good humor to be both a private virtue and a public one, as people were expected not only to strive for a pleasant spirit within themselves but were encouraged to inspire others with their own good humor, as well.

In his work on the history of jokes, Jim Holt went back even further to the time of Demosthenes in Athens, around 350 BC, to find a comedians' club that met regularly in the Temple of Heracles. It's believed that Philip of Macedon paid the comedians large sums to write down their jokes. The Romans wrote "jestbooks," the most famous of which was *Philogelos* ("Laughter Lover"), which Holt believes dates to the fourth or fifth century. Examples of these early jokes show some similarities to the forms of humor and wit that we enjoy today:

> *"How shall I cut your hair?" a talkative barber asks a wag.*
> *"In silence!"*

*A pedant was on a sea voyage when a big storm blew,*
*causing his slaves to weep in terror. "Don't cry," he con-*
*soles them. "I have freed you all in my will!"*

Notice that both examples have in common a sense of
negativity. One involves a rude person, the other insensitiv-
ity and death. As we'll see, this isn't an accident.

Humor continued to develop throughout the Middle Ages
in the form of the Arab folk tale and the first Renaissance
joke book, known as *The Liber Facetiarum*, published when
the author was 70. Humor was taken seriously enough in Old
England that the government established the Office of the
Revels in order to control this kind of entertainment. And
court jesters had an important place at the king's court, pre-
figuring the role of political humorists today, whose humor
also targets government but is played out before general audi-
ences. Sigmund Freud was particularly interested in humor,
enthusiastically collecting Jewish jokes and analyzing witty
word combinations, such as the word *alcoholidays*.

There are many examples in history of the power or, at
least, the perceived power, of humor. In Nazi Germany, for
instance, jokes were taken so seriously as a threat that telling anti-Nazi or "defeatist" jokes was a capital crime. One
popular joke from that time tells of how a Jewish father
teaches his son to say grace:

*"Today, in Germany," the father says, "the proper form of*
*grace is, 'Thank God and Hitler.' "*
    *"But what if the Fuhrer dies?" asks the boy.*
    *"Then, you just thank God."*

One particularly popular type of humor today is the
one-liner, which historian Paul Johnson traces back
to Benjamin Franklin, the first author we read in the

Vintage Readers Book Club. More generally, Johnson refers to Franklin as the "founding father of American laughs." Many of Franklin's quips still make the rounds today, including "nothing is certain but death and taxes." Other popular ones include: "He's a fool that makes his doctor his heir," "Fish and visitors smell in three days," and "Three may keep a secret ... if two of them are dead."

## What Does "Funny" Mean?

Given so much history, it may be surprising that very little is known about what makes something funny. Experts from Aristotle to Kant to Freud and others have many theories, but none that seems to fully capture the spirit of what humor is. As Freud said in *Wit and Its Relation to the Unconscious*, "When one laughs very heartily about a joke, he is not in the best mood to investigate its technique" (658). Going one step further, cartoonist Saul Steinberg sugested that trying to define humor was one of the definitions of it (Schneider, 1971).

Whatever it is, we know it when we see it, even if two people can't agree on what is or isn't funny. While the two of us often find humor in different things, we both agree with French philosopher Henri Bergson. That is, if we can transcend our daily experience enough to enable us to "look upon life as a disinterested spectator, many a drama will turn into a comedy" (1920, 3).

## The Effects of Laughter

In 1979, journalist Norman Cousins wrote the bestseller, *Anatomy of an Illness*, about how he treated himself for a mysterious inflammatory disease by watching Marx Brothers movies. His influence helped to popularize the burgeoning area of psychoneuroimmunology—an inter-disciplinary field of research that combines the behavioral sciences, neuroscience, physiology, endocrinology, and immunology. This exciting area focuses on the intimate interplay between how we think or feel and its impact on our physical functioning. While we're a long way from believing that the Marx Brothers can cure disease, there is a growing body of evidence that shows how important laughter is, not only for coping but for our physical health, too.

For example, Robin Dunbar and his group at Oxford University point out that medical patients who watch comedy videos require less pain medication than patients watching a neutral video. Dunbar believes the reason for this is that mirthful laughing, which uses different facial muscles than other kinds of laughing (such as chuckling or cackling), increases the level of endorphins—opiate-like substances that help us control pain—in our brains, in much the same way that exercise does.

Dunbar's group measured pain tolerance in two ways: they touched subjects' skin with a frozen vacuum wine cooler sleeve until they complained of pain. In the other group, they inflated a blood pressure cuff around subjects' arms until it was painful. The experimenters measured how long people could endure the pain before and after they watched one of two videos, a funny one or a documentary. For both types of pain, those who laughed in the mirthful way at the funny video tolerated the pain significantly longer than they could before having watched the video, whereas the other group had no increase in their pain tolerance.

In a 2008 study, Oswald, Proto, and Sgroi showed half of their patients a 10-minute clip of comedy sketches by a well-known British comedian, while they showed the other half a neutral film clip. Then, all patients were asked to perform the cognitive task of adding five two-digit numbers under timed conditions. Those who had seen the funny film did significantly better on the task, answering correctly 10% more of the time. In addition, all subjects were asked how happy they were both before and after the films. As we might expect, those who saw the funny film reported a higher level of happiness after the film than before.

In line with Cousins's beliefs, researchers Mary Payne Bennett and Cecile Lengacher (2006, 2008, 2009) found a relationship between watching a funny movie (*Richard Pryor Live*) and improved immune functioning, as measured by subjects' level of salivary immunoglobulin A. In another study, when compared with people who watched a neutral video, they found that laughing at a funny video led to decreased stress, as well as greater natural killer cell activity, which is another measure of immune function.

### Trying to Define Humor

The seeming impossibility of pinning down the concept of humor hasn't stopped people from trying. Some posit the superiority theory. Sometimes we find it funny to feel superior to others. In that case, a joke is funny to everyone except the person who is the butt of it. When we watch Abbott and Costello at work, say, in their famous Who's on First routine, we enjoy identifying with Abbott's superior intelligence (compared with Costello) while laughing at Costello's stupidity. At the same time, we enjoy laughing at Abbott's increasing frustration. We get to feel superior to both Abbott and Costello at the same time.

Another theory of comedy is the relief theory, which focuses on the way humor releases nervous energy. Comedian Lewis Black described comedy as, "music with tension release. You build the tension in the room, and then you release it" (Atria 2010). Freud believed humor released nervous energy by tricking the unconscious part of the mind into expressing forbidden thoughts and feelings. This is similar to journalist Michael Kinsley's description of a gaffe as a politician telling the truth.

A third explanation is the incongruity theory. According to this theory, we find humor in the unexpected or in incompatible concepts. One example is the Jewish proverb, "If the poor could die for the rich, they'd make a good living." Screenwriting instructor John Truby refers to the "comic gap" in movies in which a character has trouble completing a very easy task, for instance, the bumbling Inspector Clousseau in the *Pink Panther* films. Self-deprecating humor is another example of incongruity, suggesting humility. The incongruity comes from the expectation that people will speak well of themselves, rather than putting themselves down. Or the incongruity can come from pondering the imponderables and recognizing that just managing our lives day to day can be a huge task.

Viktor Frankl took humor very seriously. Once, he gave a colleague a homework assignment to tell a funny story every day; he and his "patient" were both inmates in Auschwitz at the time. Sometimes the men in the concentration camp barracks spontaneously put together a cabaret show, moving benches around and singing, clowning around, and telling stories. When other inmates heard about the show, they poured into the room as if it was opening night at the Copacabana. Some inmates chose to miss their daily rations of food, which were being distributed at the same time, because they considered the gathering too much nourishment for their souls to pass up.

Frankl regarded humor as a device for distancing ourselves from misery. Humor creates a perspective change—literally—as if the sufferer is now some other poor guy he's watching, rather than himself. Mindy had this experience when she recalled the most humiliating night of her childhood.

### A Visit from the New York Police Department

Mindy's teenage brother, Harry, got into a blistering fight with their mother, Clara, after he broke the rules of how to separate kosher dishes properly. In the heat of the argument, Harry mooned Clara (!), who then called the police. Four officers of the NYPD arrived within minutes.

Mindy cringed while her mother tried to explain why she had called. At first, the three men and one woman looked dazed, as if they had stepped into an episode of the *Twilight Zone*. Then, the oldest cop spoke up. "Lady," he scolded her mother, "you can't call the cops because someone put the wrong dish in the sink."

"But he showed me the tukhes!" Clara screamed back.

At the time, Mindy wished she could just disappear beneath the vinyl floor tiles. But, seen from the distance afforded by time, it was hilarious. And Mindy has been telling the story ever since.

Similarly, Vintage Reader Sue, 83, remembers a time when she was hit on the head by a tree branch. Oy. It was very painful at the time, but now, thinking about the scene makes her laugh. Joy.

This perspective change works both ways—seeing the story from a distance makes it easier to see the humor; finding it funny makes it easier to create that distance between the amused Mindy or Sue of today and their earlier unhappy versions. Perhaps the same is also true for getting distance from maladies we're currently suffering from, as if we're watching someone else's hilarious troubles instead of our own tragic ones.

In general, members of the Vintage Readers Book Club note that they find it easier to laugh as they get older. Sixty-nine-year-old Mary feels we tend to lose our childhood sense of fun as we reach adulthood and learn to censor ourselves for fear of what others might say. Now, she says, "We get it back when we're older because we care less what others think." (Note that, unlike the Ancient Greeks, Mary feels this is one of the positives of aging, rather than a negative.) Emily, 75, agrees that she cares less about her image now, but adds, "We have more experiences to draw on now, and can relate to more situations, and can appreciate the absurdities of life." It's this kind of perspective that leads Vintage Reader Renee to exclaim, "My husband and I will be married sixty years next month—if I don't strangle him first."

Perhaps this arc of learning to find more humor and absurdity in everyday life as we get older contributes to the U-bend of well-being. When 100-year-old George Burns explained that he was so old that he had to pay up front for a three-minute egg, he was doing more than being funny. He was taking what we think of as one of life's scariest subjects—death—and depriving it of its bite, twisting fear into an enjoyable moment.

Finding the humor in things adds little discontinuities to our lives, injecting moments of playfulness and fun in between the unpleasant stuff. One need only note the daily flow of jokes about aging and death to see how truly important this coping mechanism is, especially over the years. It is important to keep in mind the ways in which humor can be used to demean someone else, those who are defined as the "other," whether for racist, sexist, or ageist reasons, among others. Even so, we have come to see humor as a key virtue in life.

Jimmie's mother, Velma, found particular joy in her later years when she would collect her five "grands" around her to listen to her tales. She loved regaling them with funny stories of "the old days," which cracked them up.

## Velma's Song

Velma would sing one of her favorite songs for her grands after explaining that in the old days, people usually had all their teeth pulled at once, making it hard to eat anything that was tough, like meat. In their little town, there was a café run by a man who appreciated this problem and kept a set of false teeth in a cigar box. When a toothless customer came in asking for a steak, he would whip out the teeth from under the counter. After the customer finished eating dinner, he would carefully wash the teeth and put them back in the box for the next soul. The song is sung to the tune of *Put on Your Old Gray Bonnet* (for any readers old enough to recall how it goes):

*Put in your false teeth, Mabel,*
*Sit down to the table, and for my sake*
*Hurry and get through. For when your*
*Meal is over, you can pass them over,*
*And I'll eat my dinner too!*

Consider Judith Viorst's delightful poem that pokes fun at what aging has done to her relationship with her adult children:

### Role Reversal\*

Our children, with a touch of pique,
Complain we're out four nights a week,
And pressingly suggest we do more resting.
They offer us some dull advice
About the virtues of brown rice
And other foods we don't think worth ingesting.

---

They're urging us to sign up for
Some nice safe undemanding tour
In lieu of a far jauntier vacation,
And watch us disapprovingly
Drink every drop of our Chablis
Untroubled by their pleas for moderation.

They warn us we are sure to slip
And give ourselves a fractured hip
Unless, when climbing stairs, we grip the railing.
They tell us to slow down, relax,
Lift nothing that will strain our backs,
And take a pill for everything that's ailing.

We don't ail all that much. In fact,
We see ourselves as quite intact,
Despite some losses physical and mental.
So though we know no harm is meant,
We've come to mightily resent
Our children's tendency to act parental.

This reminds us of another use for humor. We can use it to bring up serious subjects with a light touch so that others may listen. This is what court jesters did in olden times, when they were not only allowed to criticize their masters at court, they were often expected to. It was their ability to amuse that afforded them the privilege to say things that were forbidden for others. Under enormous strain, these jesters had enough sense of self to turn a talent for comedy into a psychological and intellectual sense of power. In modern everyday life, a quick riposte is another way to feel powerful in an argument. Sometimes, we think of the witty comeback too late to use it, but we try to come up with one anyway, so that we can at least feel superior after the fact.

Today's version of the jester is the political humorist who, while meaning to entertain, also means to criticize. Comedians often do this—pointing out our foibles at the same time as they're making us laugh at them, just as Viorst uses her humor to criticize adult children who try to infantilize their parents.

We can see how humor plays a part in many of the virtues. For example, we gain new insights from listening to a joke. Humor gives us courage to transcend life's scarier moments or to express wisdom in an acceptable way. When we make other people laugh, we may give them courage to deal with life's scarier moments as well, which also helps develop our sense of humanity and our sense of being in it together. This is why the ancient Romans considered humor a public virtue as well as a private one—accepting life as it plays out, making light of things that cannot be changed, and recognizing that we all carry large existential burdens.

### More Humorous Takes on Aging

You can live to be a hundred if you give up all the things that make you want to live to be a hundred.
—Woody Allen

Life is a sexually transmitted disease and the mortality rate is one hundred percent.
　　　　　　—R. D. Laing

The best way to get most husbands to do something is to suggest that perhaps they are too old to do it.
　　　　　　—Anne Bancroft

Don't worry about avoiding temptation. As you grow older, it will avoid you.
　　　　　　—Winston Churchill

George S. Kaufman ran into an old friend at the theatre, and (reportedly) said, "My God, Peggy, I thought we were *both* dead!"

Be careful reading health books. You may die of a misprint.
　　　　　　—Mark Twain

Health nuts are going to feel stupid one day lying in bed and dying of nothing.
　　　　　　—Redd Foxx

I feel like my body has gotten totally out of shape, so my doctor sent me to an aerobics class for seniors. I bent, twisted, gyrated, jumped up and down, and perspired for an hour. But, by the time I got my leotard on, the class was over.

Reporter: And what do you think is the best thing about being 104?
104-year-old woman: *No peer pressure.*

I've sure gotten old! I've had two bypass surgeries, a hip replacement, new knees. Fought prostate cancer and diabetes. I'm half blind, can't hear anything quieter than a jet engine, take 40 different medications that make me dizzy, winded, and subject to blackouts. Hardly feel my hands and feet anymore. Can't remember if I'm 85 or 92. Have lost all my friends. But, thank God, I still have my driver's license!

An elderly woman decided to prepare her will and told her preacher she had two final requests. First, she wanted to be cremated and, second, she wanted her ashes scattered over Wal-Mart. "Wal-Mart?" the preacher exclaimed. "Then I'll be sure my daughters visit me twice a week."

I'm getting into swing dancing. Not on purpose. Some parts of my body are just prone to swinging.

It's scary when you start making the same noises as your coffeemaker.

Don't let aging get you down. It's too hard to get back up!

*The Senility Prayer:* Grant me the senility to forget the people I never liked anyway, the good fortune to run into the ones I do, and the eyesight to tell the difference.

If you don't agree with me about this, I am going to take you out of the family cemetery plot!

Remember: You don't stop laughing because you grow old. You grow old because you stop laughing.

An old man went to the doctor and asked what he could do to live longer. The doc said, "Well, you can give up alcohol, smoking, and women. You may not live longer, but it will SEEM longer."

# REFERENCES

Abbott, W. A., and Costello, L. (unknown). Who's on first? Retrieved October 10, 2013, from wimp.com/abbottcostello/

Atria, T. (2010, March 8, 2010). Catching up with. . . Lewis Black. *PasteMagazine.com*.

Bennett, M. P., and Lengacher, C. A. (2006). Humor and laughter may influence health. I. History and background. *Evid Based Complement Alternat Med*, 3(1), 61–63.

Bennett, M. P., and Lengacher, C. (2008). Humor and laughter may influence health: III. Laughter and health outcomes. *Evid Based Complement Alternat Med*, 5(1), 37–40.

Bennett, M. P., and Lengacher, C. (2009). Humor and laughter may influence health IV. Humor and immune function. *Evid Based Complement Alternat Med*, 6(2), 159–164.

Bergson, H. (1924/2009). *Laughter: an essay on the meaning of the comic.* Paris/London: Alcan/Project Gutenberg.

Cousins, N. (1978/2005). *Anatomy of an Illness: As Perceived by the Patient* (twentieth anniversary edition). New York: W.W. Norton.

Dunbar, R. I., Baron, R., Frangou, A., Pearce, E., van Leeuwen, E. J., Stow, J., Partridge, G., MacDonald, I., Barra, V., and van Vugt, M. (2012). Social laughter is correlated with an elevated pain threshold. *Proc Biol Sci*, *279*(1731), 1161–1167.

Frankl, V. E. (1963). *Man's Search for Meaning: An Introduction to Logotherapy.* Boston: Beacon Press.

Freud, S. B., A. A. (1938). *The Basic Writings of Sigmund Freud.* New York: The Modern Library.

Holt, J. (2004, April 19, 2004). Punch line: The history of jokes and those who colect them. *New Yorker*, 184–190.

Johnson, P. (2010). *Humorists: From Hogarth to Noel Coward.* New York: Harper Collins.

Morreall, J. (1997). *Humor in the Holocaust: Its Critical, Cohesive, and Coping Functions.* Paper presented at the 27th Annual Scholars' Conference on the Holocaust and the Churches, Hearing The Voices: Teaching the Holocaust to Future Generations, Tampa, Florida. http://www.holocaust-trc.org/humor-in-the-holocaust/

Oswald, A. J.; Proto, E; Sgroi, D. (2009). Happiness and productivity. *IZA Discussion Paper, 4645*. Retrieved from Social Science Research Network website: http://ssrn.com/abstract=1526075

Schneider, P. (1971). *Louvre Dialogues*. New York: Atheneum.

Truby, J. (2010). *Great Screenwriting*. Audio class. Truby Writers Studio.http://www.writersstore.com/trubys-great-screenwriting/

Viorst, J. (2005). *Role Reversal I'm Too Young to Be Seventy, and Other Delusions* (pp. 58–59). New York: Free Press.

# 7

# The Virtues of Humanity and Social Justice

## Do Unto Others

*When I was young, I admired clever people. Now that I am old, I admire kind people.*
—Abraham Joshua Heschel, theologian,
speaking to residents of a nursing home

*At thirty we are all trying to cut our names in big letters upon the walls of this tenement of life; twenty years later we have carved it, or shut up our jack-knives. Then we are ready to help others, and care less to hinder any, because nobody's elbows are in our way.*

—Oliver Wendell Holmes, The Autocrat at the Breakfast Table

One of the most famous science fiction movies of all time asks us to consider what we mean by the word *humanity*, even though it uses robots to do it. *Blade Runner*, a 1982 film based on a story by Phillip K. Dick, shows us a grim dystopia set thirty-seven years in the future. We see little sunlight; everything is in shades of gray and black. Though we see plenty of humans fighting and cheating each other, we see little humanity. The blade runners of the title are policemen hired to destroy "replicants"—human-looking robots whose superhuman strength makes them a potential threat, despite their short life span of four years. The hero is Deckard, the top blade runner, who hunts the robots one by one. "Painful to live in fear," one replicant says during the fight that ends with Deckard "killing" him.

When our hero catches up to the replicant leader, Roy, he more than meets his match. With the tables now turned, man and robot fight to the "death." At the end of the movie, the blade runner hangs from a rooftop, about to plummet, when Roy's body starts shutting down. In the film's most shocking moment, the replicant suddenly reaches out his hand to his would-be assassin and lifts him to safety before he himself collapses. The scene ends with a battered and confused Deckard trying to make sense of what just happened: "I don't know why he saved my life. Maybe in those last moments, he loved life more than he ever had before. Not just his life, anybody's life. My life. All he'd wanted were the same answers the rest of us want. Where did I come from? Where am I going? How long have I got?" Deckard learns his lesson in humanity from the nonhuman.

## CONNECTEDNESS

So, what do we mean by humanity? On one level, all it requires is, literally, to be human. But, when we speak of humanity, we usually mean much more than that. Laura Slutsky, the 63-year-old businesswoman, says, "I love that word. It brings up kindness, a global love of people, lofty ideas, caringness, givingness, a generosity of spirit." Humanity refers to a sense of connectedness, the feeling of sharing the best parts of us with each other, and even with other nonhuman species, like Laura's beloved dogs, Boo-boo and Shayna Punim. Perhaps Martin Luther King, Jr., who so exemplified this virtue, said it best: "We are all caught in an inescapable network of mutuality, tied in a single garment of destiny. Whatever affects one directly, affects all indirectly."

Our definition of humanity refers to a fellowship through which we learn to care about each other, to understand each other, and to feel responsible to and for each other. While this important virtue may sound like a vaunted concept, it is actually grounded in very concrete aspects of human achievement. Without feeling like part of a team, we wouldn't work together; we wouldn't be able to create societies or educational systems that pool intellectual resources. Working together can give us power in ways we wouldn't have realized otherwise. It's how we build bridges, discover cures for diseases, and advance society in a million different ways.

Ironically, as children, it might have been through competition that many of us initially started to learn this concept of humanity. Having an us-versus-them event reinforces the "us'ness" of us, a group with a common goal and a sense of camaraderie in reaching that goal. All the sense of a shared humanity requires is an enlarging of this circle so that we all feel like we're on the same team. The older we get, the more chances we have to find such common ground, though, it's important not to get too sentimental on this point. The older we get, the more chances we also have to see people—including ourselves—acting selfishly, and we also have to learn to protect ourselves. It's because of this difficult dichotomy that the feeling of humanity, when it's felt sincerely, can be so special and uplifting. When we know how badly we can behave toward each other, we can appreciate what it means when we behave well.

## The President of Humanity

Though we've already mentioned him a few times, it's hard not to go back to one of the most stirring examples of the virtue of humanity that took place during our lifetimes. This example embodies what humanity means and what it can concretely accomplish. When Nelson Mandela ushered South Africa into the free world, he set a very brave example for how his countrymen could learn to live together in peace. When he became president, one of his first decisions was to not fire the employees of the previous regime. Instead, he asked them to stay on and work with him. He even maintained his predecessor's personal bodyguards as his own, putting his life in the hands of men who, not that long before, would have helped to hunt him down. The men of the Presidential Protection Unit, in turn, learned to admire and love Mandela. Tony Benn, a British politician, went so far as to describe Mandela as the "president of humanity" (Carlin, 2008).

It isn't surprising that Mandela was in his 70s when he accomplished all this. He did it using his natural sense of humanity to develop strategies that would encourage others to find their own sense of humanity. Ironically, Mandela says his greatest lessons in humanity—his own and others—came from his many years in the infamous Robben Island prison, which was used for those who opposed white rule. Being treated so inhumanely strengthened Mandela's resolve to understand his enemy, not only on an intellectual level but also as human beings. Older, wiser, and armed with this knowledge, Mandela was able to encourage his enemy to do the same.

The concept of humanity is shared across time and cultures. In South Africa, it is called *ubuntu*—the appreciation that we are "all branches of the same great family tree." In Botswana, it is known as *botho*. From the ancient rabbi Hillel (Pirkei Avot, 2:5) comes a saying that can be translated as, "In a place where there are no mentsch (Yiddish for a decent human being), strive to be a mentsch." In a place where no one behaves with a sense of humanity, you must behave with humanity, and maybe the others will learn from you. Another saying of Hillel's is echoed in many different cultures around the world, also known as the golden rule—that which is hateful to you, do not do unto others.

Sometimes, it's easier to appreciate and understand this important virtue when it's lacking than when it's present. For instance, a famous case study in literature in what it means to be human, or a mentsch, or to be acting with ubuntu is that of Ebenezer Scrooge—that "squeezing, wrenching, grasping, scraping, clutching, covetous, old sinner!. . . secret, and self-contained, and *solitary as an oyster*." (Dickens 1858, 2; italics ours). Perhaps it isn't an accident that his redemption comes in older age.

And how is he described after his redemption? It is noted that "he went to church, and walked about the streets, and watched the people hurrying to and fro, and patted children on the head, and questioned beggars, and looked down into the kitchens of houses, and up to the windows, and found that everything could yield him pleasure" (96). In other words, Scrooge learned to experience himself as part of the larger world around him, a branch of the same family tree. Kindness and good deeds arose not from conscious decisions but, instead, they followed naturally because they gave him pleasure. Since Dickens's time, there has been research to back up this characterization.

For example, psychologist Elizabeth Dunn and her group (2008) have shown in many of their studies that spending money on others promotes well-being in ourselves. Whether the amount of money was large or small, people felt more fulfilled when asked to spend it on others in the form of charity or gifts for friends or family than when asked to spend it on themselves. In 2013, Lara Aknin and her colleagues observed this same relationship in 136 countries, both rich and poor. Being asked to simply remember a time when subjects spent money on others increased their sense of well-being. As Linda Moore, the 60-something writer, says, "My most meaningful experiences are anything where I'm helping a person, even in a small, concrete way."

In 2005, psychologist William Brown and colleagues looked at helping in older age adults whose average age was 75. They found that helping others in a way that cost time, money, or goods increased elders' well-being. Further, helping was associated with better health, even after taking into account the fact that different people have varying abilities to give, whether because of poor resources, health, or other factors.

## COMPASSION AND EMPATHY

So, what are some of the building blocks of this virtue of humanity? (And do they necessarily reflect the abilities of only humans?)

The first building block is compassion: the ability to feel sympathy or sorrow for others who are suffering. It's easy to think of instances when someone we love was suffering because of illness, a failure, a betrayal, or any one of life's negative experiences. One feels the pain but also the helpless feeling that all you can do is to try to share the emotion.

Compassion exists not only in people but also in the animals that came before us. Figure 7.1 shows two apes, one older, one younger. The older has just lost a fight with another adult ape. Notice his sorrow and the way the younger ape appears to sympathetically comfort his older friend.

Of course, this consolation is not necessarily something all apes do all the time. But human beings don't act with

**Figure 7.1**  A young ape consoling an older one
Reproduced with permission, photograph by Dr. Frans de Waal

"humanity" all the time, either. This is good to remember, as the way in which we might bring out each other's best self is by simply remembering that that self exists. General Constand Viljoen, one of Mandela's arch Afrikaner enemies, couldn't help but be moved when Mandela described his respect for aspects of Afrikaner culture: "[Mandela] said. . . the Afrikaner had a humanity about him. . . that if the child of an Afrikaner's farm laborer got sick, the Afrikaner farmer would take him in his bakkie to the hospital and phone to check up on him and take his parents to see him and be decent.. . .." (Carlin, 39).

Carnegie Mellon Professor Randy Pausch warned that finding the best in people is hard work. ". . . you might have to wait a long time, sometimes years, but people will show you their good side. . .. Everybody has a good side, just keep waiting, it will come out" (Pausch, 22).

Feeling compassion for someone who is suffering is one thing, but doing something about it is an even greater step in the direction of the virtue of humanity. His Holiness, the Dalai Lama notes that without the urge to actually do something to alleviate that suffering, compassion by itself feels sad, similar to the feeling of comforting a grieving person when you can't take away the source of his pain. A wonderful example of compassion in action comes from Jimmie's family.

## The Woman Who Never Met a Stranger

Jimmie's mother, Velma Coker, made friends with people wherever she went. These qualities sustained her through to age 85 when Velma was still selling insurance to people in her rural Texas community.

This outgoing quality and love of people led her to altruistic activities as well, though she didn't recognize them as being anything special. In the 1930s, when pensions finally became a reality for older people living in poverty, recipients were required to fill out documents to prove their date of birth before they could qualify. But many elderly folk, particularly African Americans, had no record of their birth, and some could neither read nor write well enough to fill out the necessary paperwork.

So, Velma would drive to their homes and ask, "Who was there with your mama when you were born? Who can we find who knows that you got born?" Then she would track down the person who could attest to their birth and help them to submit their application. She saw it as part of her obligation to people who needed help. Her philosophy was that what matters in life is what you do for your fellow man. She often said we should leave this world a little better place for our having been here.

## Tessie Hilton, 55

Tessie increased both her stress and her life satisfaction when she went back to school at age 50. Prior to that change, she was a happily married substitute teacher, leading a comfortable suburban life. When her youngest son entered high school, Tessie could see ahead to the approaching empty nest. She realized something was bothering her. Watching her elderly parents made her wonder about her own future and her connectedness to the world around her. Her parents seemed perfectly content and had a very happy marriage. But Tessie noticed they weren't particularly engaged with the outside world.

At the same time, she met other older women who, in their 80s and 90s, were vitally engaged in the world as doctors and nuns. She knew which future she preferred, so she changed course in midlife and went back to school to become a counselor. While in school, she discovered something surprising about herself. She particularly enjoyed counseling people with terminal illnesses or otherwise at the end of their lives, people who often felt cut off from the rhythms of the world outside. She found her work moving, invigorating, and much appreciated. She hopes to continue—like those who'd inspired her—for decades to come.

In addition to the ability to feel for others' suffering, we can be more helpful if we can actually empathize with their thoughts and feelings. Dr. Paul Ekman teaches new medical students, who tend to get a lot more training in understanding symptoms than in understanding their patients' feelings: "A test of your humanity is to be able to be compassionate with a patient who is afraid of something that you know there is no reason to fear. . . . Do not brush it off as not worth your attention just because you know the fear is not based in reality. . . ." (Ekman and Lama 2008, 178).

In other words, the other building block of the virtue of humanity is the intellectual ability to take the other person's point of view, to understand how things look to him or her, and to be able to have compassion for the person's feelings, whether or not you actually share them. Like the old Native American saying, to feel for someone else you must imagine you are walking in his moccasins.

Sometimes, empathy is necessarily asymmetrical, as can be the case for people from different generations. For example, Jimmie can empathize with Mindy, remembering the time when she too was 50 and sandwiched between older parents, a demanding career, and children. But the converse is not possible; Mindy cannot know yet what it's like to be 85. In fact, it is common for elders to feel the lack of empathy for their situation.

### Eddie Weaver, 80, Vintage Reader

Sometimes, I feel like children project onto their parents their own image of what an older person is like, and can't relate to how we might actually feel. For instance, suggesting, based on very meager evidence, that I shouldn't drive just because I've reached a certain age. And then, not understanding what a big deal that would be. If I'd suggested they couldn't drive just because of their age and not because of lack of ability, they would know—it's a big deal!

### Renee, 75, Vintage Reader

I have two wonderful grown sons. One thinks I can no longer do anything I used to do. And one thinks I can do absolutely everything I used to do.

They're both wrong!

Empathy sounds like such a simple word, yet it's actually a complicated feat to be able to understand someone else's perspective and see how different the world looks.

## Empathy and Mindy's Headache

As a stage II breast cancer survivor, Mindy often worries that a headache or new bump is much more than a headache or bump. When she calls her oncology team about her newest symptom, they are very careful not to belittle her fear, even as they reassure her it's nothing. "To a cancer survivor," her nurse once told her, "a headache never feels like just a headache." And it's precisely because Mindy believes her nurse understands her fears that her words have the intended comforting effect, rather than a dismissive one. More than comforting, the team's empathy is an important part of her care. If she felt patronized, Mindy might hesitate to tell them about symptoms that really do need to be examined further.

When the first replicant tells Deckard that it's "painful to live in fear," he is really trying to instill a sense of empathy in his enemy, even in the context of their brutality to each other. The robot wants the human to understand how it feels to be hunted. And when Deckard is the one being hunted by Roy, he finally does understand. Learning empathy is the first, very hard-won step to his gaining a sense of humanity.

Compassion and empathy require the ability to understand what another person is feeling and also to be capable of feeling it ourselves. This can be easier said than done, as it also involves the ability to tolerate that suffering and, if we've suffered similarly in the past, to tolerate our memories of our own pain.

## Pain, Compassion, and Connecting

When Mindy was younger, she was once rejected by a young man who preferred her pretty best friend. She was sitting alone in her parents' living room, watching some old movie on television, feeling sorry for herself. Mindy's mother, Clara, "just happened" to join her. They had always had a difficult relationship. As a Holocaust refugee, Clara often had trouble relating to Mindy's "easy" American life and pedestrian concerns.

But this time was different. Apropos of nothing, Clara spontaneously started talking about the time her own cousin stole her boyfriend from her, many years earlier. Later, Mindy's father, Archie, joined them, recounting a similar experience that had happened to him. These had never been topics of conversation before, and Mindy was profoundly moved by them. Her parents had no advice to offer but they showed her that they knew exactly how she felt, that they could empathize, and that she wasn't alone. It was the closest she ever felt to either of them, and she can still remember to this day her gratitude for their comforting words.

Linda Moore, whom we mentioned earlier, describes the change that happened when she was in her 50s, when she felt that she started to develop a greater sense of empathy with other people. Now, she says, "I'm more accepting and—this is new—I'm really interested in other people and what they think, and the ways I can contribute and offer something."

Humanity isn't only about helping people cope with life's negatives. It's also about the positives, about the joys we can share or bring people to share. Professor Pausch tells us early in his lecture about one of his main goals: "I'm a professor, there should be some lessons learned and how you can use the stuff you hear today to achieve your dreams or enable the dreams of others. And as you get older, you may find the 'enabling the dreams of others' thing is even more fun" (4).

## KINDNESS

Another element of humanity is kindness, a warm-hearted attitude that makes us want not only to alleviate suffering but also to actually bring happiness to each other. Its effects can be powerful, both for the giver and receiver of kindness. In his graduation speech at Syracuse University, celebrated writer George Saunders listed many things that he did not regret in his life, like being poor from time to time, working terrible jobs, or skinny-dipping in a river filled with monkey feces, which left him sick for months. "What I regret most in my life," he confessed, "are failures of kindness." Saunders's speech made a profound impact, and a full transcript was soon published by scores of major newspapers, blogs, and websites. "If you err," he advised the graduating seniors, "err in the direction of kindness" (Lovell, 2013).

This can be a large gesture, like Pausch's trying to help fulfill his students' grand dreams as computer scientists.

Or it can be a small one—a smile from a neighbor after a bad day at work or, as for Mindy, the jokes her friends sent her every day while she underwent chemotherapy. One thing Mandela wanted after he won the war against apartheid was to help white South Africans "feel like human beings again, like citizens of the world" (Carlin 2008, 111). Kindness comes in all forms.

As Pausch alluded, sometimes it's as we get older that we particularly enjoy helping others reach their goals. If we've reached ours, we want to share that happy experience. If we haven't reached them, as happens to the best of us, our ability to help another can feel even sweeter. We enjoy being useful. Often, it's when we're older and no longer responsible for as much, when we're not sandwiched (or panini'ed!), that we can enjoy that experience even more. Remember Nancy, the retired engineer in her 60s, and her comment: "It's time to be generative! You have to go out of your way to connect with people! I love the modern world, like technology—it makes it easier to connect."

Vintage Reader Marilyn, 67, remarked that people are often surprised when she's kind, especially younger people. One can't help but hope that an elder's kindness toward the young may kindle similar feelings in the latter, who might remember it in the next encounter with an elder. But, Marilyn stresses that it's important to give or be kind because you want to, not because you want something in return. True kindness feels special precisely because it's given as a gift, rather than a loan.

One organization that has taken great advantage of the untapped resource of elders in inner city communities is the Experience Corps (ExperienceCorps.org), a program sponsored by the American Association of Retired Persons that started in the mid-1990s. It began in Baltimore, Maryland, and has since grown to include programs in more than a dozen states. Experience Corps recruits retired midlifers and elders to volunteer their time in public schools. The children have a borrowed "grandparent" to help them read, and the older person loves helping children in need.

This expression of humanity is beneficial not only in the good feelings it engenders but in concrete ways, as well. Research shows that the children's reading improved significantly, and the elders not only enjoyed being so useful, they felt better about themselves in general. Further, a 2009 study found that the elders also had better mental functioning because of their involvement (Carlson et al., 2009).

Humanity can be experienced in quieter ways, too. Mindy can remember the early days of motherhood, how comforting it was to walk her son in his carriage through the park, and share her experiences with other exhausted new parents. They would compare the circles under their eyes, share the beautiful feelings they had that they didn't quite know how to articulate, or just describe the delicious feeling of smelling newborn skin (among the many other smells we may get from newborns). They were in it together, and big, cold, competitive New York City felt like a small friendly town.

## COOPERATION, COMPETITION, AND SOCIAL JUSTICE

This balance between cooperation and competition can yield fascinating bedfellows. One amusing example is the way three classes of computer science students at Johns Hopkins

University used cooperation to trump their professor's use of competition as a motivating force (Budryk, 2013). As was common, Professor Peter Froehlich graded on a curve, giving the student with the highest score an A and distributing the rest of the grades accordingly. This popular approach has the effect of pitting students against each other. So, the students responded in an unusual way—they agreed to boycott his exam in unison. They all showed up, as if to take the test—in case anyone broke the boycott, in which case, they all would have gone in and taken the test. But no one did. Each student stood firm and refused to take the test. As a result, they all got zeroes. Which meant that the highest grade in the class was a zero. Which meant that a zero was an A. Professor Froelich knew he was beaten and gave everyone an A.

Like the ability to console, the inclination and ability to cooperate seem to have evolutionary significance, since they don't apply only to humans. Primatologist Frans de Waal found that animals often cooperate with each other in order to get a reward. In a wonderful study titled "Elephants Know When They Need a Helping Trunk," he and his colleague Josh Plotkin found that, if they have to, elephants will work together to pull a heavy apparatus that contains food. The key phrase is "if they have to" (Plotkin et al., 2011).

The researchers connected an apparatus to a rope, both ends of which could be pulled through holes in a wall. The apparatus was on one side of the wall, the two elephants on the other, each elephant standing beside one of the holes. If only one elephant pulled on his section of rope, then the other elephant's end of the rope disappeared, and the apparatus (and the food on it) wouldn't budge. But if both elephants pulled at the same time, they could pull the apparatus close enough to the wall that their trunks could reach through the holes to get the food. This is exactly what they did. However, when one elephant got to the wall early, he did something interesting. He stepped on the rope and held it secure but didn't pull at all, allowing the second elephant to do all the work, which he did. So, freeloading is a trait not specific to humans.

In other studies, de Waal and colleague Sarah Brosnan found that animals cared about whether the experimenter was treating them fairly. When a capuchin monkey received a lesser reward than his neighbor for the same task, he literally threw it in the experimenter's face. Interestingly, there were even a few instances when monkeys refused the better reward when they saw their partners getting a lesser one (Brosnan and De Waal, 2003).

For the Dalai Lama, compassion plus courage equals social justice and altruism. When we see others' suffering and we have courage, we work to redress the world's unfairness, sometimes at our peril. Ordinary people who helped Jews and other victims of the Nazis escape the Holocaust and the many martyrs of the civil rights movement are just a few of many examples in history. Vintage Reader Joan, a 73-year-old retired social worker, points out that the phrase, "It's not fair!" resonates at even the youngest ages. "Everyone responds to a feeling of injustice."

## Larry White: Humanity Where It Counts the Most

There is a group of elders few people think about: the large number of aging prison inmates in the United

States. Larry White was one of them. After failing twice to receive parole, Larry resigned himself to his long prison sentence. As he struggled with his own depression, he became aware of the sadness of the men around him who were serving life sentences and who had no hope of any other life. He recognized that their sadness and anger didn't help their interactions with the correctional officers who were in charge of them, which made their already bad situation even worse.

At first, Larry started talking privately with individual inmates about their shared experiences. Before long, he received permission to bring the inmates together into groups to see what they could do to improve their lot. "Look," he reasoned, "this prison is your home and you're going to be living here. How can you make it better?"

Then, Larry spoke with the correctional officers and administration officials to ask for little changes the men requested, often with success. The small changes helped foster a better relationship between the inmates and the correctional officers, giving them some modicum of hope and a sense of control, even if it was limited. Slowly, the men's attitudes began to change as well. They worked together—with each other and with prison staff—to make their unpleasant home better. Over time, Larry developed his Hope Lives for Lifers project, which brings psychiatrists, clergy, educators, and others inside prison to help address inmates' concerns. He also started an educational program for elder inmates.

Larry was ultimately paroled after thirty-two years in New York state prisons. Now in his 70s, he continues his advocacy work, which includes giving workshops on what it's like to age behind bars. He refers to the men in prison as "his boys" and he feels most at home when he is working with aging lifers.

Larry and others like him remind us of the humanity of which we're all capable. The more we recognize others' humanity, the more willing and able we are to further cultivate our own. Laura Slutsky suggests that as we get older, we have a particular responsibility to help younger people develop their sense of humanity. "Young people have humanity, it's not just older people. But I think humanity grows with age, like a beautiful flower. We can teach humanity to the young. It needs to be nurtured, honored, and respected."

Perhaps Edwin Markham summed it up best in his poem "Outwitted":

He drew a circle that shut me out

Heretic, rebel, a thing to flout.

But Love and I had the wit to win:

We drew a circle that took him in!

## REFERENCES

Aknin, L. B., Barrington-Leigh, C. P., Dunn, E. W., Helliwell, J. F., Burns, J., Biswas-Diener, R., Kemeza, I., Nyende, P., Ashton-James, C. E., and Norton, M. I. (2013). Prosocial spending and well-being: cross-cultural evidence for a psychological universal. *J Pers Soc Psychol*, *104*(4), 635–652.

Brosnan, S. F., and De Waal, F. B. (2003). Monkeys reject unequal pay. *Nature*, *425*(6955), 297–299.

Brown, W. M., Consedine, N. S., and Magai, C. (2005). Altruism relates to health in an ethnically diverse sample of older adults. *J Gerontol B Psychol Sci Soc Sci*, *60*(3), P143–152.

Budryk, Z. (2013, February 12, 2013). Dangerous curves. *InsideHigherEd.com*.

Carlin, J. (2008). *Playing the Enemy: Nelson Mandela and the Game That Made a Nation.* New York: Penguin Press.

Carlson, M. C., Erickson, K. I., Kramer, A. F., Voss, M. W., Bolea, N., Mielke, M., McGill, S., Rebok, G. W., Seeman, T., and Fried, L. P. (2009). Evidence for neurocognitive plasticity in at-risk older adults: The Experience Corps program. *J Gerontol A Biol Sci Med Sci*, *64*(12), 1275–1282.

Davis, A. (Ed.) (1980). *Pirkei Avos: A New Translation and Anthology of its Classical Commentaries.* New York: Metsudah.

Dickens, C. (1858). *A Christmas Carol.* London: Bradbury and Evans/ Google eBooks.

Dunn, E. W., Aknin, L. B., and Norton, M. I. (2008). Spending money on others promotes happiness. *Science*, *319*(5870), 1687–1688.

Ekman, P., and Lama, D. (2008). *Emotional Awareness: Overcoming the Obstacles to Psychological Balance and Compassion.* New York: Henry Holt and Co.

Fancher, H., Peoples, D. W., and Dick, P. K. (writers) and R. Scott (director). (1982). Blade Runner [Motion Picture]: Warner Bros.

Holmes, O. W. (1873/2013). *The Autocrat of the Breakfast-Table.* Boston: James R. Osgood & Company/Project Gutenberg.

King Jr., M. L. (1964). *Letter From a Birmingham Jail: Why We Can't Wait* (pp. 85–110). Boston: Beacon.

Lovell, J. (2013, July 31, 2013). George Saunders's advice to graduates, Web. *The New York Times*.

Pausch, R. and Zolotow, J. (2008). *The Last Lecture.* New York: Hyperion.

Pirkei Avot: Sayings of the Jewish Fathers. (2005). Translated by J. I. Gorfinkle. Public Domain Books.

Plotnik, J. M., Lair, R., Suphachoksahakun, W., and de Waal, F. B. (2011). Elephants know when they need a helping trunk in a cooperative task. *Proc Natl Acad Sci U S A*, *108*(12), 5116–5121.

Stengel, R. (2009). *Mandela's Way*. New York: Crown Archetype.

# 8

# The Virtue of Courage

## If I Only Had the Nerve

*Courage is the most important of the virtues,*
*because without it, no other virtue can be practiced consistently.*
—Maya Angelou, to Cornell University class of 2009

*A ship in harbor is safe.*
*But that is not what ships are built for.*
—attributed to John Shedd, *Salt from My Attic*, 1928

The Greeks saw courage as one of the primary virtues of the good life. Courage and fortitude can come in the face of an external threat, such as threat to life, as in a battle, or it might be courage to face a prolonged threat, such as a grave illness. Another type of courage comes not from an external source but an internal one: the moral strength to stand up for a conviction or a belief that might lead to adverse consequences. The sacred texts of many religious traditions abound in stories of fortitude in the face of overwhelming threat. Courage doesn't require fearlessness, rather, it refers to the ability to live with our fears while we try to move past them.

The stories in this chapter remind us that courage is seen at all ages. Some people seem to be born with courage, while others develop this virtue over time, a process often helped by years of dealing with adversity. The idea of losing a loved one, for example, might seem totally unimaginable. Yet, when it happens, courage emerges from some surprising inner source to permit us to cope with it. Courage can be contagious, inspiring the same in others as well as inspiring a sense of humanity and faith in the good that people are capable of.

## Inspired by Others' Bravery: Mindy, September 11, 2001

Mindy will never forget the sound of the sirens on the fire trucks and police cars as they raced through her neighborhood to get to the World Trade Center on 9/11. The men and women in those trucks and cars were the ones who ran into buildings everyone else was running out of. Mindy had planned to be on the Observation Deck of one of the towers that morning with her older son, Max, who was 5 at the time. But, because it was his first day of kindergarten, they decided to delay their trip until late morning. Thanks to this twist of fate, they were nowhere near the site when the planes hit.

In the aftermath of the attack, Mindy couldn't stop thinking of their close call and was terrified even to walk on the streets of her Upper West Side neighborhood, afraid of imaginary bombs or what, exactly, she didn't know. Every time she went outside, she felt terrified, especially when she was with Max or his baby brother, Isaac.

But Mindy kept thinking of those sirens and those brave men and women who fought every human instinct for self-preservation in order to help those in need in the Twin Towers. If they had the strength to walk into those buildings and up those many stairs, she could muster the strength and force herself to walk down the street. After she walked them enough times, her terrors finally subsided.

### *Just Doing What Needs to Be Done*

People do not usually describe themselves as courageous. When was the last time you heard someone say, "I was so courageous"? Rather, most courageous souls don't realize what they're capable of until a situation occurs that requires courage. Then, we surprise ourselves by rising to the challenge. But even then, we might not recognize our actions as anything out of the ordinary.

### Wesley Autrey: Courage Begets Humanity

On a January afternoon in 2007, Wesley Autrey, a 50-year-old New York City construction worker, was waiting for the subway at the 137th Street Station in Upper Manhattan. Suddenly, a young man standing next to him started to have a seizure. Autrey tried to help him, but the young man stumbled across the platform and fell onto the tracks. Autrey could see the lights of an oncoming subway train approaching and dove onto the tracks, hoping to pull the young man to safety before the train reached him. But there wasn't enough time. So, Autrey threw himself over the man in a drainage trench between the rails and pushed down. The train's operator saw the two men and applied the brakes, but, by the time the train came to a stop, five of the subway cars had already passed right over them. The train passed so close to Autrey that his cap had grease marks from the wheels. Amazingly, they both survived.

"I just saw someone who needed help," Autrey later told the *New York Times*, "I did what I felt was right."

Mayor Michael Bloomberg awarded Autrey the Bronze Medallion, describing him as an inspiration to the world and reminding us that we were all surrounded by everyday heroes. In 2007, President George W. Bush honored Autrey in his State of the Union Address and quoted the hero: "We got guys and girls overseas dying for us to have our freedoms. We got to show each other some love."

### Profiles in Courage: John F. Kennedy, 1943

In the foreword to her father's book, *Profiles in Courage*, Caroline Kennedy provided some details of his breathtaking courage in 1943 when he was a lieutenant in the Pacific during World War II. Kennedy's PT boat had been rammed and destroyed, leaving two dead and only him and a badly burned colleague alive. Despite serious back injuries, Kennedy swam three miles to a Japanese-held island in the Solomons, while dragging his friend by clenching the man's life-jacket strap between his teeth. Over the next six days, they hid during the day, and Kennedy swam at night to seek help. When he found two friendly islanders, they gave him a coconut on which he carved a message indicating their location. The islanders took the message to a hidden Australian lookout who arranged for a rescue mission that saved their lives.

QUIET COURAGE OVER THE YEARS

Courage is also about fear and how we manage it. It isn't just facing one moment of fear but consistently facing each new crisis—and determining what to do. In fact, the root of the word *crisis* is neither negative nor positive; it comes from the Greek word "krinein," which means "to decide." Sometimes, it isn't individual moments of crisis that teach us courage. Instead, someone's unacknowledged courage can be honed over a lifetime of difficult experiences.

## George Dawson: Life Is So Good

George Dawson displayed tremendous courage by simply going to school. He was 98 years old when he took the plunge and decided it was time to learn to read and write. In fact, his was a life full of quiet courage in the face of desperate circumstances.

In *Life Is So Good*, the book he later co-authored with writer Richard Glaubman, Dawson describes being the oldest child of a poor African American family in northeast Texas in the early twentieth century. George took it as his lot to work from an early age on the farm so that his younger siblings could go to school. He worked hard, first on farms, then railroads. He married and had several children whom he encouraged to get a good education.

George managed to keep his illiteracy a secret until his children were in high school. Years later, when he was 98, an adult education recruiter invited him to attend a class. He accepted the challenge. By the time he turned 101, George had become a model for the class. Reading at a third grade level and aspiring to get his high school equivalency diploma, he also inspired the other students to try to keep up with him. He became a national figure as word spread about the country's oldest student. His courage and fortitude spawned a remarkable wisdom and generosity of spirit. Despite all that he went through and all that he was deprived of, Dawson says, "Life is so good."

Jimmie grew up in the same area of Texas that George did, only a few years later and in much more comfortable circumstances. Like George, she also looks back and says, "Life is so good and I wouldn't change it." But, for George, at 101, to feel it after a lifetime of hardships, seemed remarkably generous and forgiving. What Dawson achieved was more than learning to read—his story also inspired countless others to face their own fears and venture into new territory at any age. Stories like his inspire others at all ages to open their minds to possibilities they had never considered before.

The story of courage in ordinary life that is closest to Jimmie's heart is that of her father, Clifford Coker, who had the strength simply to be himself.

## Clifford: The Courage to Be Yourself

Clifford Coker had an unerring moral compass that reflected the strength of his character. Never one to talk much about his beliefs, his actions showed his quiet bravery. He was born, grew up, and died in a small rural Texas community that prized its strong fundamentalist religion and did not tolerate nonbelievers.

Yet Clifford defied the ministers' emotional entreaties at the annual revival meetings and weekly services, pleading with him to declare his faith or suffer eternal damnation—pleas impossible for most to ignore, but not for Clifford. He loved singing the hymns and he supported the little church in every way he could. He helped maintain its cemetery where his family was buried. And he helped to buy a generator that supported a lighting system to permit evening services—though it often failed and left the congregation in the dark, to the great pleasure of the children.

Regardless of the many ways he supported the church and its community, however, Clifford stayed true to his own personal philosophy of life. It is hard to imagine now the strength it took for him to maintain his lonely stance year after year in the face of the social pressure. Now, almost one hundred years later, that strength still inspires his daughter.

## COURAGE, FEAR, ORDINARY PEOPLE, AND EXTRAORDINARY CIRCUMSTANCES

In what may be the first truly American fairy tale, *The Wonderful Wizard of Oz,* written by Frank Baum and illustrated by W. W. Denslow, introduced a century's worth of children to the Cowardly Lion. And the famous lion is very "cowardly," indeed. Yet, this does not stop him from helping his friends fight spear-throwers, flying monkeys, and even a very wicked witch. The wizard famously teaches him, "There is no living thing that is not afraid when it faces danger. True courage is in facing danger when you are afraid, and that kind of courage you have in plenty" (223–224).

## Humanity Begets Courage: Zofia Banya and Israel Rubinek

In war-torn Poland in 1941, Zofia Banya was a poor farmer's wife who did not have enough money to pay for the items she needed from Israel Rubinek's dry goods store. "Not to worry," he told her. She could have the items and pay him back when she could. Nobody offered credit during those lean times, and Zofia never forgot Israel's act of kindness.

This was very fortunate for Israel, as, two years later, when the Jews of his town were being deported or executed, Zofia sent word that Israel and his wife, Frania, could hide on her farm. Despite the constant danger of being caught and executed herself (and over her husband's initial objections), Zofia hid the couple for more than two years, saving their lives.

Banya and Rubinek wouldn't see each other again for forty years, when the Rubineks returned for an emotional reunion. The Rubineks' son, actor Saul Rubinek, filmed the reunion for the documentary *So Many Miracles*. "I felt so much pity for them," Zofia says in the film, "it was impossible to betray them."

## Clara: A Mother's Fear Inspires a Daughter

Mindy's mother, Clara, was only 6 years old in her native Rumania when the fascists took over. She had to leave school, and would never get a formal education. Young Clara and her family joined the Jewish partisans, who helped them hide in the forest for the next two years. She never thought of herself as brave. Quite the opposite. She was terrified all the time, whether fleeing Nazis or townspeople eager to turn in her and her family, or being smuggled across borders. Years later, when she came to America as a newlywed, she did not know the language or even a soul other than her husband, Archie (also a refugee), She was terrified to leave her family. But she went. Just ten months later, she became a mother with no other family to help her. By the time Mindy's younger brother was born two years later, Clara was speaking English like a pro.

Clara has remained a symbol for Mindy of what people are capable of surviving and of moving past, fear or no fear. Seventy years later, Clara no longer forages for leaves big enough to cover herself at night. Instead, she lives with Archie with a roof over their heads, in Brooklyn, New York. Sometimes, she has new things to fear. But she survives them, as she'd survived so many times before.

In 2006, when Mindy was first diagnosed with breast cancer, she, too, was terrified. And it gave her enormous comfort and strength to think of the things her mother had made it through. Thinking how her parents' years in the war were now a distant memory, Mindy was able to look forward to the day she could say the same about her cancer and cancer treatment.

Personal stories of people brave enough to reveal their most difficult problems and how they coped remain a major way in which we learn from each other. Each time we face a fear, the courage branch on the oak tree grows a little bigger. One can look back and gather strength from past decisions. When more crises occur as we grow older—losses, illnesses—we can look back and take a certain pride in surviving. Perhaps this is one of the secrets of the right side of the U-bend of well-being. With age comes the ability to say, "With all I've been through, why should I be afraid? I will just face what I have to when I have to. In the meantime, I am going to make the best of it."

### Helen Cantor: I Came Out of My Shell at 70

Helen would certainly never have thought of herself as courageous. She started out quite lonely, growing up in a home with a strong mother who was much closer to her older sister than to her. She felt unworthy of praise and was socially awkward as well. Helen did better as she got older, and decided to become a nurse. Graduating from nursing school went a long way toward improving her self-confidence; she loved her patients and the medical setting, and her colleagues and patients loved her right back. But she remained painfully shy, especially with men, and often struggled with depression. She never married.

Helen always regretted not having had a family, though she continued to love her work and find great purpose in it for many years. When she was 70, her sister died, which seemed to liberate Helen from being the lesser daughter, leading her to "come out of my shell at 70." She became even more self-confident and successfully took on the care of her sick mother, first at home and then in a nursing home.

Helen lived in the same studio apartment for many of her 93 years. She takes great pride in keeping it in good condition and attractive, despite the fact that she is legally blind. She had many friends over the years and regularly went to plays and musical events until her vision diminished. However, she still walks around her neighborhood with the aid of a walker and does her own grocery shopping. If she needs help reading the labels, other grocery shoppers are only too happy to read them for her.

In addition to her many other activities, Helen is also a member of our Aging and Illness support group and the Vintage Readers Book Club. Her hilariously incisive comments are often the ones that are most remembered by group members. She says it is now unusual for her to become depressed, and she tries to stay busy. She is as good as Google when it comes to knowing about resources for elders, staying up to date thanks to the many books, magazines, and newspapers on tape that she receives from the Library of Congress.

Helen describes having had to adapt to changing situations in her life and growing along the way. When asked about death a few years ago, she said, "I can't worry about next year. Look, I don't want to die. But I'm 90 years old—if I died tomorrow, I'd be set. My papers are in order, my will and all that. Only, I just got four chairs recovered in my apartment. I want to stick around at least to see how they look with the new covers."

COURAGE CAN START VERY YOUNG

Courage can be expressed at any age. Elders often find particular comfort in stories of bravery in the young. They instill hope for the future of the world that the older generation is passing on to the younger.

## Ruby Bridges: The Bravery of a Child

Ruby was only 6 years old when she helped integrate New Orleans grade schools in the 1960s. She was in first grade and she had to be escorted to and from school daily by four armed federal marshals, a scene that was immortalized in the famous painting by Norman Rockwell (Figure 8.1). The marshals walked her from the car to the school for the entire school

**Figure 8.1** Norman Rockwell's painting of Ruby Bridges
Printed by permission of the Norman Rockwell Family Agency
Copyright 2014 the Normal Rockwell Family Entities

year; she was jeered and screamed at every morning before she went inside. She was the school's only student, since the other parents kept their children home in protest.

Ruby spent her school days with the federally mandated teacher and received the same abuse outside the school when she went home. This went on for the full school year, yet Ruby never stopped going. Psychiatrist Robert Coles got to know Ruby and her family, as he was studying the impact of desegregation on the children of the South. He found that she complained little and seemed to tolerate the stress well.

One day, the teacher mentioned to Coles that Ruby seemed to be talking to the crowd, which made them look even more menacing. When he asked Ruby about it, she explained that her parents had told her about Jesus and how he had prayed for the mob around him, so she did the same.

"I was talking to God," she said, "I was praying for the people in the street . . . I say please forgive them because they don't know what they are doing" (Coles 2010, 128).

Courage comes packaged in small bodies sometimes. And Ruby in her white dress, shoes, and white hair ribbon stands as an example of courage in action, as she tolerated unimaginable abuse day after day while never losing her sense of humanity and hope.

Together, Bob Coles and Jimmie saw the courage of young people facing paralyzing and life-threatening polio in the summer of 1955. As young psychiatry residents at Massachusetts General Hospital, they were witness to the last major epidemic of poliomyelitis prior to the advent of the Salk vaccine. They were both interested in how young, otherwise healthy people faced such serious illness. Suddenly, their hospital emergency room was flooded with people whose symptoms ranged from minor weakness in a limb to paralysis extending up to the neck. These patients were placed in a large ward constructed to hold twenty iron lungs—large cylinders that encased their bodies, with their heads outside, that pushed air in and out to expand and contract their rib cage, thus breathing for them. To be healthy one day and totally paralyzed the next was catastrophic.

Yet, these young adults found ways to adapt and to cope with their situation. They were incredibly brave, often cheering each other up. Their down periods came, but they found courage within themselves to carry on. One of the most satisfying aspects of working in medicine is the way it reveals the strength of character that people have in reserve that can surprise even themselves.

We often think of teenagers as being particularly reckless, rather than brave or courageous. Yet when facing crises, they show admirable character strengths.

### The Courage to Hope and Cope: Sheila Kussner

When Sheila Kussner was only 15 years old, she developed a sarcoma on her right leg above the knee that required amputation of the whole leg. Now age 80, she can still remember how hard it was to look and feel so different from the other teenagers. This was at a time when there were no psychological resources to help kids cope with illness. Cancer was a word not spoken but whispered, if that. Her parents took the position that she was perfectly normal and should behave that way—and she did.

Sheila realized how isolated amputees were and she began visiting with recent amputees in the hospital to give them the peer support she hadn't received. As the years went by, she gathered friends to join her to form Hope and Cope, now an organization of several hundred volunteers who provide free services for cancer patients, including the Wellness House and many supportive activities.

## ALL THOSE DECISIONS THROUGH THE YEARS

Ultimately, it takes courage to be yourself at any age and to face the challenges that come with each phase of life. Young people must decide by age 17 about: college? no college? a gap year? to do what? what will be waiting down the line, socially, economically, technologically? While young people have a sense of the world ahead, they aren't necessarily confident or assured that they will be able to meet an unknown future. And yet they start building those futures, just the same.

Decisions take even more courage when the carefree (to some degree) college years end and we hear, "Oh my gosh, what will I do in the real world? I have to grow up." And most do, though there is a T-shirt that says, "I must grow old, but I don't have to grow up." There are Peter Pans among us whose bravado may mask a high level of fear.

Young and middle-aged adults are bombarded by discussions that require courage: Do I marry? Do I have/want children? How can I manage my job and move up the career ladder with a family to care for? Why are my parents looking so frail? Then comes even more need for courage: How do I climb back down this career ladder and get off and retire? Who will I be then without my identity as a teacher, engineer, doctor?

Character has been showing through all along, directing those decisions. Over time, it has helped create the context of our lives in which we've found loving relationships and met challenges in carrying out meaningful tasks. Eleanor Roosevelt summed it up well in her book, *You Learn by Living*: ". . . we shape our lives and we shape ourselves. The process never ends until we die. And the choices we make are ultimately our own responsibility" (Roosevelt 1960, 2).

Now that people are living longer than before, there is increasing interest in an act II or career II, especially for those sixty-plus years. But that can happen even earlier in life. Tessie Hilton, mentioned earlier, is a wonderful example of someone who raised four children and had the courage to start something totally new when she turned 50 and her youngest began high school.

Of course, what seems like courage in our earlier years may look quite different in our later years, simply because we don't always stay afraid of the same things. For example, the Vintage Readers have found that speaking their minds—even when others disagree—is now simply less scary than it was when they were younger. Knowing what we want and what we don't want can take a lot of courage when we're younger, especially if there are so many experienced people telling us we're wrong. The art of *traveling light* makes it easier to do these "courageous" things because they no longer require as much courage. When we're younger, it can be hard to imagine what we'll be able to accomplish later because of our lessened sense of fear.

Whether because of increasing courage from facing adversity or less need for courage, we would do well to have some faith in ourselves, both for who we are now and who we will be in the future. As Christopher Robin tells his beloved companion, Winnie the Pooh, in the film *Pooh's Grand Adventure*: "Promise me you'll always remember you're braver than you believe, and stronger than you seem, and smarter than you think."

## REFERENCES

Baum, L. F., and Denslow, W. W. (1900). *The Wonderful Wizard of Oz*. Chicago: George M. Hill Company.

Buckley, C. (2007, January 3, 2007). Man is rescued by stranger on subway tracks, Web. *The New York Times*.

Coles, R. (2010). *Handing One Another Along*, T. Hall and V. Kennedy eds. New York: Random House.

Dawson, G., and Glaubman, R. (2000). *Life is Good*. New York: Random House.

Ju, A. (2008, May 24, 2008). Courage is the most important virtue, says writer and civil rights activist Maya Angelou at Convocation, Web. *The Cornell Chronicle*.

Kennedy, J. F., and Kennedy, C. (2004). *Profiles in Courage*. New York: Harper Collins.

Milne, A. A., Geurs, K., and Crocker, C. (writers) and K. Geurs (director). (1997). Pooh's Grand Adventure: The Search for Christopher Robin [Video]: Walt Disney Television, Buena Vista Television.

Roosevelt, E. (1960). *You Learn by Living*. New York: Harper.

Rubinek, S. (Writer) and K. Smalley and V. Sarin (directors). (1987). *So Many Miracles* [Documentary Film]. In S. Rubinek (producer). Canada: National Center for Jewish Film.

Scrivener, L. (2009, December 20, 2009). A simple act of kindness saved lives, Web. *The Toronto Star*.

Shedd, J. A. (1928). *Salt from My Attic*. Portland: Mosher Press.

# 9

# The Virtue of Wisdom

## Knowing What We Don't Know

*We are not provided with wisdom, we must discover it for ourselves,*
*after a journey through the wilderness which no one else can take for us,*
*an effort which no one can spare us.*
> —Marcel Proust, *Within a Budding Grove*

Like courage, wisdom represents a goal or an ideal to be pursued, rather than a quality people recognize in themselves. Most people, especially older people, will modestly declare that they do not consider themselves wise. In saying so, they are following the tradition of Socrates who, ironically, took pride in saying he had no wisdom, even though his definition of wisdom included a sense of humility and acceptance of the limits of one's knowledge. Indeed, if we thought we already knew all there was to know, we wouldn't be open to learning new things or coming around to new insights.

### THE VINTAGE READERS READING LIST

We didn't start the Vintage Readers Book Club to be a venue for the world's wisdom; we started it because we thought it would be meaningful and fun. In our support group, members tended to focus on themselves and their immediate problems. Many were living alone, with an aide or family member, and they lacked the physical ability to become actively involved in community activities—they were "stuck" in their problems, and getting intellectual stimulation was difficult. They were bright, productive, creative people who would like to talk with others about ideas, but they lacked the motivation to find a forum in which to explore them.

We began to study the wisdom of thinkers from long ago, focusing on the Greek idea of the virtues. Interestingly, the subject of age rarely came up. Usually, it was the subject of "Life with a capital L" that came up, even though most of the group ranged in age from 60 to 90 plus. We have since read from such classics as the *Meditations* of the Roman ruler Marcus Aurelius; St. Augustine on memory (coupled with Nobel laureate Eric Kandel's work); Plutarch's letter to his wife; and many others. Sometimes, we deviated into more contemporary territory, such as when we compared the Declaration of Independence with Martin Luther King Jr.'s 1963 *Letter from the Birmingham Jail*. Our discussions about the courage of the founding fathers, on the one hand, and this remarkable man, on the other, were inspired and, well, "wise." (A full list of our readings can be found in appendix.)

Group attendance is remarkably high—higher than for the original group from which we'd spun off! And there's no dearth of intellectual stimulation, as our discussions have been highly animated. Some members even bring in notes. Possibly, the most important outcome is how much the Vintage Readers enjoy thinking beyond themselves and their immediate situation, even though those personal issues manage to come up in the context of our discussions of the virtues. Discussion is noisy, all have ideas and want to talk and often laugh. When our time is up, few people leave, no one wants the conversation about these universals of the human condition to end.

The second important benefit of the group's enthusiastic sharing of ideas has been more social than intellectual. Aside from reducing the problems of spending too much time alone, the group helps members feel like a part of something larger than themselves, both as part of the group and as part of the larger world of people who wonder about the same universal questions that they do. Even when they can't attend individual meetings, group members have told us how they've kept up with the readings, nonetheless. Sometimes, they call in and join the discussion that way. The Vintage Readers Club continues to evolve, and other centers are inquiring about it on behalf of their older members. We joke that at our age we are unlikely to read all fifty classics, but that does not dampen enthusiasm to start and try. Knowing when you have a good thing—isn't that an example of wisdom, too?

## MORE WISDOM THAN ANY OF US HAVE. . . .

The 1980s saw a burst of interest in research on wisdom, not just from a philosophical perspective. Psychologist Robert Sternberg undertook to capture the state of information on scientific research on wisdom and asked key researchers from around the world to weigh in. In the opening chapter of his book, *Wisdom: Its Nature, Origins, and Development*, he notes: "To understand wisdom fully and correctly requires more wisdom than any of us have. . . . And if we are to believe the authors of the chapters in this book, the recognition that total understanding will always elude us is itself a sign of wisdom" (3).

We can see how humbly researchers in the field perceived their task. Wisdom is a particularly elusive concept, in part, because it isn't a simple virtue but, rather, a multifaceted way of living, thinking about, and evaluating the world. How is it different from intelligence, for instance, or shrewdness? Is it possible to be wise and evil at the same time? And what is the relationship between wisdom and age? Is it "older and wiser"? Or is there "no fool like an old fool"?

## WISDOM: IS A DEFINITION POSSIBLE?

One approach to studying wisdom has been for researchers to ask people to name individuals whom they considered to be wise. Then, the researchers would study those people and identify the attributes they had in common. For Jimmie, the first person who came to mind as an example of wisdom, long before she started wondering about how to define the term, was the same man whose quiet courage had inspired her for all these years, her father, Clifford.

### Wisdom Isn't Learned in School

Clifford grew up on his father's farm in northeast rural Texas in the early 1900s. His formal education at a country school stopped at the end of ninth grade. Like

Socrates, Clifford would never have described himself as wise, but he had a strong sense of carrying on his father's respected tradition as a man of the soil. He inspired confidence despite his absence of "book larnin'," and his "horse sense" more than made up for it.

He farmed the black land, as his father had done, learning from experience and "the school of hard knocks" how to rotate the cotton, corn, oats, and pasture to conserve the soil. He managed sheep and cattle and kept mules to pull the farm equipment until tractors took over the job. During the Depression, Clifford milked eight to ten cows daily to raise extra money. Each day, the milk had to be collected in big containers and lowered into their well to stay cool until picked up by the local dairy. Jimmie and her mother made butter and took it to town to sell at 25 cents per pound.

Clifford was a quiet, patient man who spoke little unless he clearly had something to say. He was totally honest and fair. His handshake was his bond. Like many farmers, he borrowed money from the county bank each spring to make the crop and then repaid it in the fall after harvest, with the hope that there would be more income than out-go (not always the case). That depended a great deal on the price of cotton and the presence of just the right amount of rain.

Several families lived on Clifford's farm to help with work, particularly the cotton crop. Many signed their names with an X because they could not read or write, but they all knew they could trust Clifford to keep accurate books about their work hours.

He knew he wanted a better education for Jimmie than he'd had, this at a time when most parents didn't take higher education for girls very seriously. Together with Jimmie's mother, Velma, Clifford sacrificed so that Jimmie could go to college and then to medical school. He never traveled, never flew in a plane, but he had a keen interest in the one public school and its improvement, and he served on its board. He worked tirelessly to bring paved roads and electricity to the rural area. As a result of his efforts, Jimmie was able to fly in many planes and go to many places to get the word out about a subject she felt was getting short shrift in medicine— the psychological needs of cancer patients.

It's easy to see why Clifford's maturity, kindness, and strong sense of right and wrong remained beacons for Jimmie. But what do his qualities have to do with wisdom? A lot. To understand how, let's look at the research literature a little more closely.

## WHO IS WISE?

In 1990, psychologists Lucinda Orwoll and Marion Perlmutter looked at different ways to study wisdom. One method is to study the attributes of people designated as wise by others. Another approach is to explore how laypeople define the term. Table 9.1 lists some of the descriptors that were identified in the various studies.

While the descriptions of wisdom are not identical, they overlap a great deal, despite the different approaches. The general consensus is that wisdom involves the ability

**Table 9.1** Overlapping descriptions generated by three studies of implicit theories of wisdom

| Clayton and Bitten | Sternberg | Holliday and Chandler |
|---|---|---|
| Understanding Introspective | Understands people<br>   Knows self best<br>Thoughtful<br>Fair<br>Good listener<br>Admits mistakes<br>Listens to all sides of an<br>   issue | Understands people<br>   Understands self<br>Thoughtful<br>A great listener<br>Learns from<br>   experience<br>Considers all points of<br>   view |
| Knowledgeable Observant | Huge store of knowledge<br>Perceptive<br>Sensible<br>Thinks before acting or<br>   making decisions<br>Can take the long view<br>Thinks before speaking<br>Seeks out information,<br>   especially details | Knowledgeable<br>   Observant/<br>   perceptive<br>Uses common sense<br>Thinks before<br>   deciding<br>Cares about<br>   consequences<br>Has foresight<br>Sees the larger context<br>Discreet<br>Curious |
| Experienced | Experienced<br>   Age/maturity | Experienced<br>Mature/older |
| Intuitive | Has intuition<br>Can offer solutions based<br>   on truth and fairness<br>Can read between the<br>   lines<br>Can understand<br>   and interpret the<br>   environment | Intuitive<br>Moral<br>Sees essence of<br>   situations<br>Evaluates information |

(*Continued*)

**Table 9.1** Continued

| Clayton and Bitten | Sternberg | Holliday and Chandler |
|---|---|---|
| Empathic | —— | Empathic |
| Intelligent | | Intelligent |

(Adapted from Orwoll, L., & Perlmutter, M. The study of wise persons: integrating a personality perspective. In R. J. Sternberg (Ed.), Wisdom: Its Nature, Origins, and Development. Copyright Cambridge University Press 1990. Reprinted with the permission of Cambridge University Press.)

to make good decisions in uncertain situations. First, people described as wise tend to have a high degree of self-insight, that is, they understand themselves. They also are highly empathic and caring and have a good understanding of other people. These qualities are coupled with a broad perspective of the world, with concerns about global and universal themes. And, while all researchers find a level of knowledge to be an important part of wisdom, they are not necessarily referring to formal education but to the kind of "horse sense" Clifford gained from just living and learning.

## WISDOM AND AGING

More recently, Igor Grossman and colleagues at the University of Michigan, looked at the different definitions put forward about wisdom. They, too, found the concept to be too elusive for a simple definition. However, in reviewing the research, they described six dimensions that came up most frequently:

- The ability to see events from multiple perspectives
- The ability to seek and find solutions based on compromise
- The ability to deal well with uncertainty
- Flexibility to make predictions and decisions about the future
- Recognize that change is a part of life
- The ability to search for ways to resolve conflicts

When the researchers looked at the relationship between wisdom and age, they found something very interesting. The researchers had people of all ages read accounts of two kinds of social conflicts: 1) between groups (for instance, two ethnic groups in Tajikistan with different philosophies about tradition versus modernization) and 2) between individuals (for example, adult siblings arguing over paying for their deceased parents' headstone).

The participants were asked what they expected would happen next and why. Their responses were graded on each of the six dimensions of wisdom, as well as on a composite score. Those in the 60- to 90-year-old group won hands down. When it came to conflicts among groups of people, they had the highest scores on every dimension of wisdom as well as on the composite score. When it came to the conflict among siblings, the oldest group again had the highest composite score and the highest score on four of the six dimensions (perspective, acceptance of change, flexibility, and compromise).

The researchers determined that, at least in the area of understanding and trying to resolve social conflict, older is, in fact, wiser. They recommended that for this reason, elders should be included in more negotiations of social conflicts, echoing Cicero's essay recommendation that older adults should continue to serve in the government so that their sense of prudence might counterbalance the impulsive decisions of the "hot-tempered" youth.

It should be noted that the researchers also found that some aspects of thinking decreased with age in the groups studied. For example, older people tended to be more easily distracted and to drift in conversation. Indeed, these are attributes that can come with age. Another common complaint of older age is memory loss or not being able to think of the right word. This is a mild, common condition many people encounter as they get older, known as benign forgetting disorder of older age. Such "senior moments" may be irritating but, as Grossman and his colleagues point out, they don't get in the way of true wisdom.

Laura Carstensen and her colleagues at Stanford suggest that it isn't only time and the accumulation of experience that account for this kind of wisdom. She argues that with age comes greater motivation to find a sense of meaning in life as well as less motivation to expand our personal horizons. The resulting perspective is likely to lead to more thoughtful, wise decisions. The ability to grow lighter as we go is a form of wisdom that entails learning how not to sweat the small stuff, learning how not to be too invested in particular outcomes (for example, being the "winner" in an argument), and accepting that while it's worth aspiring to important goals, we won't always achieve them.

## WISDOM AND BENEVOLENCE

One additional asset that is implied by all this research is the sense of benevolence that we think of when we think of wise people. In the long run, resolving difficulties is ultimately in our own best interests, as a life of peace and stability is much more pleasant than one in which we're always feeling that we have to outsmart the next guy. And a life in which we pool our resources to help each other build, invent, and heal is likely to be a better life. In other words, exhibiting the virtue of humanity is not only humane, it's also wise.

Maybe this is why Eleanor Roosevelt felt that maturity, wisdom, and benevolence went hand in hand. For her, the mature person is one who: ". . . does not think only in absolutes, who is able to be objective even when deeply stirred emotionally, who has learned that there is both good and bad in all people and in all things, and who walks humbly and deals charitably with the circumstances of life, knowing that in this world all of us need both love and charity" (63).

This maturity includes the widening of our social radius that Erikson described, from a narrow one in childhood (our primary family) to a broader one in adulthood, as we head new families. Moving into older age, we tend to think beyond our own selves and finite life by having greater concern for the generations to follow and the quality of the world they will live in. Elders begin to think more often about the future of the physical environment of the planet and about preserving the social values in our society. This is similar to Dr. Hedda Bolgar's feeling described earlier of being connected to anything alive, whether people, animals, or plants.

At the same time, the challenge is to see ourselves through our own lens. Vintage Reader Anne-Marie suggests that elders sometimes cause their own problems by buying into the ageist images others place on them. As Lillian, 93, told us, "I didn't start to feel old until other people started to treat me that way."

Eddie Weaver, 80, notes that the younger generation tends to project its fears onto the older one. But Ann-Marie says it doesn't matter what other people think of her; what matters is how vital she experiences herself to be. Staying "me" means understanding the context we live in, while remembering both who we are and who we are not, and caring less about living up to—or down to—others' expectations.

William May relates wisdom in older age to this ability to react less strongly to life's disappointments and inconsistencies. The Vintage Readers seem to agree. "You need to learn to expect less from people as you get older, to let go. Sometimes, we need to let the younger generation off the hook."

Ironically, staying "me" sometimes means adapting to changes in our situations by making changes in ourselves as well. To do this wisely means to understand what we want.

## Revisiting Tessie Hilton: Recognizing the Need for Change

When Tessie went back to school at age 50, she didn't do it lightly. She had thought hard about what she wanted out of life, not only at that time but in the future. When her youngest child was in high school, Tessie realized that he, too, would soon follow his siblings out of the coop, and she wondered how she would take to an empty nest. So, she did what many people do—she looked to her parents to see how they handled this change in life. An affluent couple (as are Tessie and her husband), her parents seemed to handle that transition very well, enjoying each other's company, playing golf at their country club, and living a very comfortable life.

On reflection, Tessie noted two important lessons she learned from her mother, Abigail. One was that it was important to treat others well and to be a nurturing force in the world. This was something she had always wanted to emulate. The other was that Abigail's whole world seemed to be her husband. What would happen, Tessie thought, if Abigail outlived him? Further, Tessie realized she wouldn't be content with a similarly insular lifestyle. She had a strong sense that she had had an unusually comfortable and easy life and felt she should give back in some way.

So, Tessie emulated the parts that felt positive to her and looked to other kinds of elderly role models for ways she might feel vital and of use to the world, especially as she got older, like a nun she knew who was still ministering to the sick and the poor in her 80s. At age 50, Tessie started a new career as a religious counselor. To her surprise, she particularly enjoyed working with people who were seriously ill or dying. Now, she is counseling terminally ill patients and their families about their emotional and spiritual needs. Five years later, she is more than happy with the change she made and feels a sense of fulfillment and meaning she hadn't felt before.

The change Tessie made seems virtuous in many senses—particularly in the courage it took to make such a change, and the humanity to want to in the first place. It is also a wonderful example of the wisdom required to know herself—who she is, who she wants to be, and how she wants to feel. It was empathy that enabled her to work with people in great distress and that gave her the ability to look at people who were happy in their context—her parents—while recognizing that that context wouldn't be right for her. Perhaps the greatest clue to her wisdom is how happy she continues to be now, living for the past few years with the choices she made.

Sometimes, wisdom means having the insight to know you want your context to change as little as possible, even when change is forced on you. And the ability to adapt.

## Eddie Weaver: The Wisdom of Continuity in the Face of Change

Eddie Weaver had a brilliant career as a physicist at a technology company. Retirement was not something he wanted or even considered until it was required at age 70. Immediately, he started thinking through what he might do next. A man with a keen intellectual curiosity, he was not about to move into a rocker. Eddie organized a graduate program in engineering at a local college, then led it through several years of successful development. But his ideas and interests were even broader than engineering.

A few years ago, when we were starting to develop our supportive counseling program for older people who were coping with illness, we asked Eddie to join our expert panel. He continues to come up with ideas for programs to help elders. He is the "go-to guy" when it comes to finding the best hearing aids. And, for elders who are more intimidated by technology, he can help to find a simple computer without all the bells and whistles, that they can use comfortably.

Eddie also continues to participate in our groups and is a founding member of the Vintage Readers Book Club. Always engaged, despite whatever new ailments pop up, Eddie had to start phoning in to meetings when his wife took ill. And yet, he continues to read the assigned readings carefully and always contributes thoughtful comments as well as suggestions for future readings.

One of Eddie's chief complaints about retirement is that he misses the intellectual exchange he used to have with colleagues during his working days. So he continues to seek out opportunities to talk with peers about the subjects he is interested in. He joined a community of ROMEOs (really old men eating out), who have lunch together regularly and chat.

## THE WISE MOMENT

As we noted, few of us would describe ourselves as wise, even those (or especially those) whom other people describe as wise. But we can all recognize that there have been moments or situations in our lives when we were, indeed, wise. And it is important to remember to do so; after all, we learn not only from our mistakes, but also from our achievements. And even a slight achievement can yield great results.

## Mindy and Max

When Mindy was pregnant with her second child, her older son, Max, was 4 years old. He "knew" that when the baby came in a few months, it would be cuter than he and that Mindy and her husband, Rob, would abandon him. His parents promised they would never do such a thing. Max's response was, "Thank you. But you're just trying to make me feel better. I know you're lying." And he would cry inconsolably.

Max decided he was going to beat his family to the punch and run away from home. Mindy vigilantly watched the front door. One day, during one of Max's crying spells, Mindy broke down, crying miserably, too. The best she could do through her sobs was to apologize for not knowing how to help him feel better and to promise him again that she was telling the truth and that she and Rob would always love him.

Suddenly, after Mindy's outburst, everything started to change. Max didn't seem that miserable anymore. He still talked regularly about running away, but he stopped crying and didn't bolt for the front door. It seemed the issue had passed. Until one day, when Mindy was in the final month of her pregnancy and they were walking home from the bookstore. Max suddenly stopped in front of the steps of a random brownstone and declared, "This is the home I'm running away to. Bye." With that, he turned and walked up the steps without looking back.

Mindy had no idea how to react. Her back hurt and she couldn't muster the strength even to waddle up the steps to get him. So, she stayed where she was and said, "Okay." She started to walk in the direction of their home, hoping he'd follow her. He didn't.

After an initial moment of terror, Mindy decided to walk back to the foot of Max's "new family's" home and said in a friendly voice, "You know, I'm really going to miss you. Do you think you could stay with us at least a little longer before you leave so we can hang out together a little bit more?"

Max thought a little and then chirped, "Okay!" He joined Mindy on their walk home, and never tried to run away again. When his little brother, Isaac, was born a month later, his parents were finally able to prove that Max was as loved as ever. And it helped that Isaac adored Max from the moment he was born. The deal was sealed a year later when Isaac said his first word—Max.

Mindy still remembers that moment of terror when she didn't know what to do while watching Max walk up those stairs. She didn't analyze what it was about her strategy that worked, but she still remembers the quiet feeling of triumph from her moment of wisdom. It came in very handy during those many times when she would feel less competent at handling her children's needs or even general social situations. And she would remember how a light touch may be the best approach.

Mindy was reminded of this experience again when the Vintage Readers were reading *Aesop's Fables* and talking about the life lessons they found most important. Renee, 75, remarked on the importance of expecting less from her adult children as time went on. The others agreed. Expecting less meant less conflict and more independence. Even if that meant they felt they sometimes gave their children more than they got back. It is the way things work, they felt.

But the group went further. Changing our expectations also means giving because we want to give, not because we expect something in return. It's the giving that feels good. And if they've learned anything through the years, it's that life is too short not to do the things that feel good. That's a hard-earned piece of wisdom in itself.

## REFERENCES

Carstensen, L. L. (2006). The influence of a sense of time on human development. *Science*, *312*(5782), 1913–1915.

Carstensen, L. L., Pasupathi, M., Mayr, U., and Nesselroade, J. R. (2000). Emotional experience in everyday life across the adult life span. *J Pers Soc Psychol*, *79*(4), 644–655.

Cicero, M. T. (1820). *An Essay on Old Age*. Translated by W. Melmoth. Google Ebook.

Grossmann, I., Na, J., Varnum, M. E., Park, D. C., Kitayama, S., and Nisbett, R. E. (2010). Reasoning about social conflicts improves into old age. *Proc Natl Acad Sci U S A*, *107*(16), 7246–7250.

May, W. (1986). The virtues and vices of the elderly. In T. R. Cole and S. A. Gadow (eds.), *What Does It Mean to Grow Old: Reflections from the Humanities*. Durham, NC: Duke University Press, 41–61.

Orwoll, L. O., and Perlmutter, M. (1990). The study of wise persons: Integrating a personality perspective. In R. J. Sternberg (ed.),

*Wisdom: Its Nature, Origins, and Development.* Cambridge: Cambridge University Press, 160–177.

Proust, M. (1919/1998). *Within a Budding Grove*, C. K. S. Moncrieff and T. Kilmartin, trans. New York: Modern Library.

Roosevelt, E. (1960). *You Learn by Living.* New York: Harper.

Sternberg, R. J. (1990). *Wisdom: Its Nature, Origins and Development.* Cambridge: Cambridge University Press.

# 10

# The Virtue of Temperance

## Moderation in All Things (Almost)

*Mastering others is strength;*
*mastering yourself is true power*
—Lao Tzu, *Tao de Ching 33* (sixth century BC)

Words go in and out of fashion, and, in the United States, temperance has been out since the Prohibition era when Carrie Nation led the Temperance Movement, wielding her axe and destroying beer barrels. However, the idea has been around for a long time. The Greeks identified temperance as one of the four cardinal virtues (along with courage, justice, and humanity), defining it as moderation in thought, feeling, and action. In fact, they believed that no other virtue could be practiced without temperance.

If we look at some of the virtues we have discussed so far, we can see the Greeks' point. You may remember that "President of Humanity" Nelson Mandela thought his greatest strength was his ability to learn to control his emotional responses to provocations. Without that, he couldn't have dealt with his prison guards, let alone negotiate the end of the war or the beginning of the ensuing reconciliation.

Temperance was important to Mandela in another way, as well. Misplaced generosity or too much empathy with the other side might have interfered with his ability to stand his ground and fight for what he thought was right. True temperance, in other words, is always a balancing act, even when it comes to exercising the other virtues—not too much, not too little. Too much courage, and we might behave rashly, putting ourselves and others at risk. Too little ability to temper our fears, and we might not be able to persevere. Wisdom also requires the ability to recognize this balance: if wise people are too forceful in stating their opinions, even if they're correct, other people might resent them and consider them arrogant; if they aren't forceful enough, they're dismissed. Even temperance itself should sometimes be tempered. Life isn't much fun if we're always in control and never letting loose; we might miss out on new and valuable experiences. Jimmie's friend once cautioned her, "Don't forget to leave room for serendipity."

In general, though, our ability to avoid excess—whether in our emotions or our behaviors—is central to our survival as a society. It's no surprise, then, that the idea of temperance—or its more modern-sounding equivalents, self-control, willpower, and self-regulation—has been at the heart of many religious teachings throughout history, from Buddhism to the Judeo-Christian tradition. In earlier times, intemperate behaviors were often thought of as vices or sins and were to be avoided at all costs, if one wanted to escape eternal damnation in the afterlife. Even when it came to this life, physicians going back at least to the time of Galen associated temperance with a better old age, as we saw in chapter 3. Remember Cicero's warning that lack of temperance in our earlier years often hands a ravaged body over to older age. Though the specifics differed, moderate diet and exercise were always at the top of the list. They often included prescriptions for emotional temperance, too, like trying to control feelings of anger and regret.

Like internal physical mechanisms that alert us when necessary, for example, when our bodies need food or our blood sugar is too low, the virtue of temperance serves as a mental barometer for our feelings and actions, alerting us when they are leaving the moderate zone. It provides an internal alarm system that signals us to take care in how we're balancing our desires, feelings, and responsibilities. We often think of self-control in terms of our behaviors, like drinking too much wine at dinner or going to the movies instead of washing the dishes. But before the behavior comes the feeling— "I really feel like seeing a movie"—or the thought—"But those dishes aren't going to clean themselves. Remember how hard it was to get rid of those roaches?" How well we heed the danger signals starts in our hearts and our heads. That's why we'll discuss temperance in hearts and heads before we tackle self-control of our actions.

## SELF-REGULATION OF OUR THOUGHTS AND FEELINGS

*To enjoy good health, to bring happiness to one's family, to bring peace to all, one must first discipline and control one's own mind.*
—Buddha

As individuals, we learn how to manage this balancing act over a lifetime of experiences. Carstensen's group found that older adults have better emotional control and that when they do feel bad, as we all do at times, they tend to be less upset by their negative emotions than younger people. Developmental psychologists Carol Magai and Beth Halpern suggest that our multiple "sandwich" roles in midlife may be particularly helpful in this respect. They force us, by necessity, to learn to regulate our emotions in order to navigate the demands of those competing roles. Audrey, a 67-year-old retired professor, comments that age has helped her to "master my emotional intensity. Now, I'm more in control because I've studied life a long time. I'm less overstimulated, less reactive. I have greater compassion, taking things less personally." There are many ways we can practice the kind of emotional restraint Audrey talks about, particularly prudence, forgiveness, and humility.

## PRUDENCE

Prudence refers to self-regulation over the long haul and usually requires a sense of farsightedness. It is easy to see why people often associate it with the virtue of wisdom and the accumulation of insights gained from earlier life experiences that guide our current actions. Being older helps. It is easier to delay short-term pleasures for long-term gain if we have a long-term view. Often, the easiest way to have a long-term view is to have lived long enough to see the consequences of the things we did when we were younger. When we asked the Aging and Illness Group how their perspective had changed since their younger days, Buddy, a 75-year-old retired chemist, said, "I didn't *have* perspective when I was younger." As Oliver Sacks wrote in a *New York Times* op-ed, "At 80, one can take a long view and have a vivid, lived sense of history not possible at an earlier age."

The sandwich generation is prime time for learning this quality. Life at that time often seems like one conflicting goal after another, between caring for children and/or parents, careers, and our own personal needs. There are often few, if any, decisions that are easy or clear-cut.

### Jane: Prudence Today, Fulfilling a Dream Tomorrow

Jane was a retired teacher who married young. She always wanted to learn to play piano, but her parents couldn't afford lessons. As an adult, she had children soon after marrying. Her husband left her not long after their third child was born. With three young children to provide for and raise, she had neither the time nor the money for lessons or practice. The welfare of her children was the more important immediate goal.

But that didn't mean Jane had to give up her dream. While she fulfilled her obligations to her family, she recognized that her musical goals could wait for her "when I retire, I will. . . ." And she did just that, to her delight and that of her family and friends. Jane had done her job, taking care of her children and managing her career. Now, her retirement years took on new meaning, as she could focus on her goal in a way she could never have done when she was younger.

Prudence requires a delicate balance between different wants and needs. Jane wanted to learn to play well but she also wanted to give her children the attention they needed. It is interesting that the ability to delay gratification and persevere can be seen in some children from an early age. It's a character trait that serves them well. Jimmie's mother, Velma, loved to tell her the story of John, Velma's 9-year-old nephew.

## John: What Does It Mean to Want Something?

In the early 1900s, John learned to play the ukulele and sing. He was so talented that he was asked to perform on the radio.

"John," Velma asked him, "what's the secret of how you did it?"

"Ya gotta want to," John explained. "Ya gotta want to a whole lot, to work hard and practice, even when you DON'T want to."

John had the idea from the start that just the feeling of wanting wasn't enough. He had to balance his wanting other things—to play ball or hang out with friends—against his desire to master the ukulele. His reward was to sing on the radio.

### SELF-CONTROL BEGINS IN CHILDHOOD

While many of us get better at adapting as we age, there is a great deal of research that shows long-lasting benefits to practicing self-control and moderation early in life. Of course, that's the time when many of us least want to practice those things. But the earlier we practice and the earlier we teach our children to do the same, the better we (and they) can handle life later on.

Evidence for this was provided by Walter Mischel and his colleagues at Stanford and Columbia Universities; they explored preschoolers' ability to delay gratification using a simple treat. A researcher met with each child individually, placing a marshmallow (or a different treat, if the child preferred) in front of her. The researcher then explained to the child that he was about to leave the room for a few minutes and presented her with a choice: if she could wait until he returned, she would get two marshmallows; if she couldn't wait, she could ring a bell, and he would return immediately, but she would get only one marshmallow. He then left the child alone to see if she managed to wait and be rewarded with the extra marshmallow.

Ten years later, the children's parents were asked about their children's general ability to control themselves. Those children who had been able to wait for the extra marshmallow years before were now less distractible, more likely to control themselves in frustrating situations, and less likely to yield to temptations. They also performed better academically.

A large longitudinal study of 1,037 children was reported by Terrie Moffitt and an international team. They followed a group of children from when they were toddlers to when they were in their 40s, examining their level of self-control and its relation to health, economic status, and criminal record over a thirty-two–year period. The children represent all the children born in a single city, Dunedin, New Zealand, in a given year. Remarkably, the study retained 96% of its subjects.

Moffitt and colleagues noted that normally among the first things we demand of our children is to control their impulses and modulate how they express their emotions.

For instance, we try to get them to use their words rather than throw tantrums. That's because their ability to practice self-control will largely determine how they will do in school, community, and, finally, in society as adults. Moffitt and her colleagues gathered data on the children's behavior at ages 3, 5, 6, 9, and 11. The researchers then assessed health, economic status, and criminal records when the participants were 32.

Strikingly, they observed a self-control gradient in which both boys and girls with less self-control when younger were later more likely to have worse health and economic status, and were more likely to commit crimes. These differences started to appear when participants were in their adolescence. Children who'd been found to have low self-control when younger began smoking earlier and were more likely to abuse drugs, leave school early, and to have unplanned pregnancies. The differences between the highest and the lowest scoring groups were extreme: 3% of the high self-control group had multiple health problems compared with 10% of the low self-control group; 26% of the high self-control group became single parents versus 56% of the low self-control group; and when it came to criminal convictions, the difference was 13% versus 43%.

In a study of 245 adolescents from disadvantaged homes who had experienced chronic stress, Carissa Low and her colleagues found that coping styles could have a physiological impact. They looked at subjects' levels of C reactive protein, which is elevated when there is tissue damage. Low and colleagues made the following distinction between two styles of problem solving: positive engagement, which involved self-control (subjects endorsed statements like "You try to figure it out on your own" or "You try to improve yourself,") and disengagement (for example, "listen to music," "eat food," "get angry," and "yell at people.")

Those with the positive style had less evidence of tissue damage than those in the disengaged group. Despite the fact that they all came from chronically stressed and disadvantaged homes, those who had greater self-control experienced less negative physiological impact.

Experts believe that self-control can and should be taught early to children in school. But future research needs to identify the key ingredients and how to make them available. These early interventions might help reduce adolescent "mistakes." Later, adolescent education could reinforce the earlier lessons to fortify children for adulthood. This is a time when the ability to keep in mind long-term goals would help them meet career goals and have satisfying, stable relationships. Cicero would approve of these interventions, which would help our younger selves hand over a sounder body and more prudent mind to our older selves.

## SELF-REGULATION AND FORGIVENESS

It is normal to be angry when we feel mistreated in some way or hurt by someone who is dear to us. As children, we learn early that hitting isn't allowed, and some time later, we understand that "meltdowns" do not get us what we want. But learning how to forgive is a deeper process that takes more time. It also requires the ability to temper some of our more intense and angry emotions. Without this capacity, we might find ourselves very lonely; over time, no close relationship, whether with family or friends, is without hurts that need to be overcome if the relationship is to survive.

Forgiveness involves an acceptance, which may mean different things to different people. Some will say, "I can forgive but not forget." Others describe it as "letting go" rather than "forgiveness." Regardless of the method, the key ingredient seems to be the ability to control our emotional responses. Without control, anger can lead to the desire for vengeance or retribution, ranging from carrying a grudge, to avoiding or punishing the offender, to fantasies of violence, or even to violence itself.

Some research suggests that elders tend to be more forgiving than their younger counterparts. It may be that life's experiences allow us to see the value of forgiveness. Philosopher William May suggests that's because as we get older, we learn to lower our expectations about people and goals. As the Vintage Readers put it, "We accept less more graciously."

Laura Carstensen and her colleagues also propose that the awareness of living within a shorter time frame puts pressure on maintaining—or reestablishing—relationships and therefore to letting go of anger. Sometimes that means setting things right before it's too late. This is important for the elder's peace of mind. Especially since, as we'll see in chapter 12, loneliness can be particularly difficult to deal with as we get older. It can be important for middle aged children of elders, too, especially as their parents join the ranks of the oldest old.

In 2013, Swedish psychologist Mathias Allemand and his colleagues went so far as to develop a "forgiveness intervention" to help elders resolve painful hurts from the past. Older subjects attended a group session that focused on understanding a hurtful memory. The sessions reduced their ruminations and sad feelings, helping the elders to see those experiences from a more tolerable perspective in which they forgave without losing their sense of self-respect.

This intervention also utilizes the virtue of humanity, helping elders find reasons to empathize with the people who they feel have wronged them. The ability to put ourselves in others' shoes helps us to forgive them, just as we're sometimes the transgressors who ask for others' forgiveness. Even in situations where the elder couldn't bring himself to forgive, the intervention aimed to help him "overcome unforgiveness" and control his anger or desire for vengeance.

## Hugh: Forgiveness From Our Children

Hugh was a bright 93-year-old widower who prided himself on his intellect. He expected and demanded a great deal from his only child, Mary. Mary was dutiful but not particularly intellectual and never was able to hold a significant job. She was gentle and overly passive in work situations, holding lower-level jobs that Hugh ridiculed. Both father and daughter felt bitter toward each other.

In the course of his work with Jimmie, Hugh started to understand and accept that his daughter wasn't capable of meeting her father's high expectations, though she had tried. In one family session, Hugh was moved to ask Mary's forgiveness for his harshness. Mary was moved to tears, grateful that her father had finally accepted her for who she was, rather than his fantasy of who he wanted her to be.

## Audrey: Forgiveness for Our Parents

Audrey's parents were very glamorous when younger, and she often felt neglected as a child. By the time her mother reached her late 90s and started needing more of her daughter's help, Audrey started to feel resentful. "Here I was having to take care of someone who used to make me feel abandoned, even though I was in her presence."

"But now, over time," Audrey reports, "I can see her appeal. She's fun, but she's just not reflective. I'm a reflective child of nonreflective deniers (her father, much older than her mother, had died years before). She has 'life wisdom'. I know we love each other. I no longer feel tormented."

Of course, we see examples of forgiveness in the face of anger at all ages. Ruby Bridges, for example, was a model of forgiveness, which allowed her to maintain her courage as she withstood verbal abuse day after day on her way to school during desegregation.

Perhaps, when forgiveness isn't forthcoming, a little humor can do in a pinch. Like the old joke about the prim, 90-year-old woman sitting in the front pew at church listening thoughtfully:

The minister asked, "Please raise your hand if you would like to ask forgiveness for any problems you have caused others."

All hands went up, except that of our prim gray-haired lady. The minister asked, "Why wouldn't you want to ask forgiveness?"

"I don't have to," she answered. "I've outlived all the bitches."

Forgiveness must extend to ourselves as well, especially in older age when we have a long list of memories of things we wish we had done differently. As we find ourselves forgiven by others for our own transgressions, we learn to forgive ourselves, too. Without that ability, it would be hard to navigate our regrets over past actions and escape the feeling of despair. Since we all have regrets, putting them in a context we can live with is an important part of adapting to the later stages of life.

## SELF-REGULATION AND HUMILITY

*The fly sat upon the axle-tree of the chariot wheel and said,*
*"What a dust do I raise!"*
                    —Aesop's Fables

This area of temperance has many descriptors: humility, modesty, self-effacement. Its opposites are self-importance, arrogance, and vanity. The quality of modesty doesn't get much traction in a society like ours, which often overvalues the individual and rewards tooting your own horn (since no one else is likely to toot it for you). Some of our most beloved figures are known for their modesty and generosity of spirit, such as Eleanor Roosevelt, Mother Theresa, and Gandhi. While ordinary modest people may not attract much attention in the bigger world, they are likely much appreciated by those around them for that very virtue. We do complain about the people who are self-centered and show it by pomposity, boasting, and arrogance.

While our society does not condone arrogance, however, neither does it seem to particularly value modesty. How likely would you be to vote for a political candidate who acknowledged that she didn't know the answer to all the community's problems? Which doctor would you prefer: the one who speaks with authority about how he'll definitely fix your problem or the one who honestly admits not knowing all? We like to think that the arrogant politician will get his come-uppance at the polls and that the doctor's honesty will be appreciated by the discerning person as the stronger position. But that isn't always the case.

The clever put-down of boastful braggarts is still alive and well, and perhaps no place is it better used than in Jimmie's home state, Texas. She still calls on these droll sayings when the situation demands it. Like the short and sweet put-down for a self-inflated rancher: Big hat, no cows. She also recalls how Congressman "Mr. Sam" Rayburn put fellow politicians in their place: "Who does that guy think he is? He puts his pants on one leg at a time, just like I do." Another homespun favorite is, "You can cook your boots in the oven but they won't come out biscuits." Plain old people, just like plain old boots, remain the same no matter how they try to pretend otherwise.

Many "plain old people" do amazing things all the time without caring about any fanfare. We often don't know about them, precisely because of their humility. But if we think about it enough, we can probably come up with examples of people quietly doing wonderful things on a regular basis.

### Tom: Just One Person Trying to Help Another

One of Jimmie's colleagues at Memorial Sloan Kettering is remembered—and beloved—for his humility. Coupled with a delightful sense of humor, this virtue made him unforgettable. Tom McDonnell is presently a retired Maryknoll priest who also trained as a psychologist. When he came to work at Memorial, he explained that he preferred to work with the hospital patients at night, because that's "when the 'demons' come out."

Tom made his nightly rounds in the intensive care unit, where patients often found it particularly hard to sleep, not to mention the anxious families at their bedsides and in the waiting rooms. Tom had a disarming, light and playful way of talking about himself, the church, and God that put people at ease. He often made them laugh at him and themselves, as well, though he was able to change his stance quickly when a prayer or a more serious discussion was needed. The patients and families appreciated his humble style. He never acted like an all-knowing religious representative, rather, he was simply one human being trying to help another.

One particularly moving example of Tom's self-effacement occurred one night when he tried to comfort a young Jewish mother who was praying for her young son. The mother became upset when her son's yarmulke slipped off his head and fell behind his bed. Appreciating the symbolic importance of the yarmulke staying on the boy's head—in Jewish tradition, it is a sign of humility, a reminder that God is always above—Tom immediately dropped to his hands and knees, crawled under the bed, retrieved the cap, and gently placed it back on the boy's head. Tom's act comforted the distraught mother, and they prayed together for the boy's life.

### Sister Elaine: Just Doing What She Loves

Another colleague at Memorial who is notable for her humility is Sister Elaine Goodell, an 87-year-old nun.

She appears bright and early in the presurgical unit at Memorial at 4:45 a.m. so that she can greet patients waiting their turn to go into the operating room. She has a cheery word for all and a prayer for those who want it.

Sister Elaine has done this for more than thirty years and would never consider stopping. She seeks no reward or even recognition for her humanistic work. She says simply that she loves what she does.

Of course, people couldn't help but notice Sister Elaine's quiet selflessness, despite her modesty. In 2009, the HealthCare Chaplaincy, which represents more than twenty institutions, presented her with their Wholeness of Life Award.

## MODERATION IN OUR ACTIONS

*If I had known I was going to live this long, I'd have taken better care of myself.*
—Euble Blake on his 100th birthday (Kaufman, 1993)

When we first started working on this section, we were a little wary, not wanting to be thought of as modern-day Carrie Nations, wagging our fingers about how important it is to moderate our behavior and live "right." And we have to admit, there's a lot of research presented in this chapter that may also feel a little like being told to eat your spinach and broccoli. Mindy, for one, much prefers chocolate to spinach. As we'll see, though, it really makes a difference in our lives, especially as we start getting older and, hopefully, continue to do so for a long time.

Peterson and Seligman (2004), quoting Baumeister et al. (1996), note that problems in self-regulation are central to nearly all the personal and social problems that currently plague citizens of the modern, developed world. Even the short list includes the following: "drug addiction and abuse, alcoholism, smoking, crime and violence, unwanted pregnancy, sexually transmitted diseases, underachievements in school, gambling, personal debt, credit card abuse, lack of financial savings, anger and hostility, failure to exercise regularly, and overeating" (506).

This statement is quite an indictment of overconsuming, self-indulgent societies in which the ability to moderate our behaviors seems weak to absent. This issue is particularly important when we're older, especially now that so many of us are living into our 80s, 90s, and even 100s and have to deal with the consequences, as Eubie Blake suggests. But self-control is important for our well-being at any age.

## SELF-CONTROL AND HEALTH BEHAVIORS

Failures in personal self-regulation have had an enormous impact on our health and on how much it costs to maintain it in our society. Figure 10.1 shows a graph published in a 2007 article in the *New England Journal of Medicine*. In that article, Dr. Steven Schroeder reported that a full 40% of premature deaths in the United States were related to behaviors—more than genetics, the environment, or social circumstances.

Perhaps it's no wonder that while we spend more on health care than any other nation in the world, the United States ranks near the bottom on most standard health measures. In 2004, among 192 nations, the United States ranked forty-sixth in average life expectancy from birth. We would have thought these data would have aroused more of an outcry, especially since Schroeder pointed out that "the single greatest opportunity to improve health and reduce

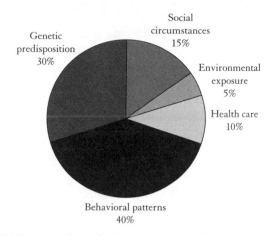

**Figure 10.1** Proportional contribution to premature death

From We can do better—Improving the health of the American people, Schroeder, S. A., Vol. 357, p. 1222. Copyright (2007) Massachusetts Medical Society. Reprinted with permission from Massachusetts Medical Society.

premature deaths is in personal behavior" (1222). In other words, better self-regulation saves lives.

Figure 10.2 illustrates the most common behavioral causes of premature death. Smoking, obesity, and inactivity lead the field by far, with alcohol next on the list. Car accidents, guns, drugs, and sexual behavior constitute the rest. While we're smoking less than we used to, tobacco use still kills almost half a million people each year, with smokers dying fifteen years earlier, on average, than nonsmokers.

At the personal level, we have developed programs to help people quit smoking through counseling and medication. Many people have stopped smoking, even after decades of cigarette use. One amusing sign we've seen in

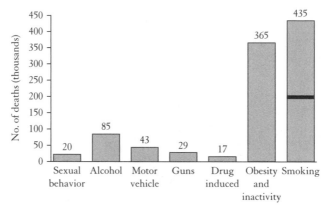

**Figure 10.2** Behavioral causes of death

From We can do better—Improving the health of the American people, Schroeder, S. A., Vol. 357, p. 1223. Copyright (2007) Massachusetts Medical Society. Reprinted with permission from Massachusetts Medical Society.

our department reads, "If at first you don't succeed, quit, quit again!" On the community level, we have made great strides by making public places smoke-free and by raising taxes to increase the cost of smoking in order to increase the incentive to quit. Schroeder points out that the success of antismoking campaigns as well as the remarkable increase in seatbelt use in cars (which rapidly reduced accident fatalities) show that it is possible to change our behaviors on a large scale. So, we have good reason to be optimistic.

The successful approaches used in many smoking-cessation programs suggest that similar personal interventions have the potential to help decrease overeating, obesity, and inactivity. As Schroeder points out, there are intriguing social similarities between obesity and smoking:

- Both usually start in adolescence.
- Both became more common in the last century.

- Both involve aggressively marketed products.
- Both are more common in poorer groups.
- Physicians in both cases have been slow to incorporate education and treatment into routine medicine.

When it comes to smoking, much education has been directed toward children who, in turn, often put pressure on their smoking parents.

As far as a healthy diet is concerned, there is now a similar initiative in schools to provide healthier school lunches as well as information about physical fitness; awareness of foods' calorie content and of ingredients in fast foods is also on the rise. This gets transmitted over time by children to their parents. Outside school, restaurants have been pressured to inform the public about calorie counts. Addressing children first is doubly helpful because it helps information trickle back to parents and because good habits begun early will lead to benefits enjoyed over decades of a person's life. These kinds of initiatives are good examples of how people can benefit from community help. Similar initiatives are being studied in particularly disadvantaged groups.

## HEALTH BEHAVIORS IN DISADVANTAGED GROUPS

It is a sad but real truth that the behavioral risks for premature death fall disproportionately on the poor and disadvantaged, which often include the elderly. They die earlier and with more disabilities, regardless of race. It is here that the personal and societal issues intersect. Having fewer resources can make it harder to moderate diet, for example; buying fast food is cheaper and saves time. And working two or three jobs doesn't leave much time for getting in a good exercise regimen. But, given the consequences, it's important to try, just the same. Even if it's too late for an adult, it isn't too late for children to establish good habits early in life in order to help stave off chronic health problems later.

Investigators in England have led the way by addressing these issues directly. The Whitehall studies, begun in 1967 —initially, covering all male civil servants in London and later including women—showed a remarkable gradient of health by social class: the lower the social class, the higher the mortality and the poorer the person's state of health. Diet and exercise were identified as particular risk factors (Stringhini et al., 2012).

Subsequently, these social scientists led the way in efforts to educate large groups of disadvantaged people about obesity and exercise. They adapted their social policies regarding the key issues that impact health, namely, poverty, poor housing, low income, and greater environmental stresses. It remains to be seen how successful they will be. Schroeder points out that in the United States, we have not addressed health issues from this broader perspective. Instead, we tend to look at health problems in terms of race and specific diseases. Unfortunately, this approach blurs the impact of social class and poverty and makes it harder to address some of the real problems that underlie the data.

Another cultural complication in the United States regarding health behavior is that personal behaviors are indeed personal, and many fight loud and vigorously for the right of the individual to eat or drink as he chooses. Whether or not new regulations will improve our health, they can make people feel as if Big Brother is interfering.

While this isn't a simple issue, the data show that the stakes involved in intemperate behavior can be very high, and we will have to come some distance to find common ground on such important issues in public health.

## Appalachia: A Community Approach

One interesting approach to studying obesity in the context of significant health disparities is an ongoing research effort by Electra Paskett, a health psychologist at the Ohio State University. She is studying strategies to educate underserved groups in Appalachia—those with low income, poor education, and poor health— about ways to fight obesity and cancer by teaming up with trusted community resources. She is collaborating with area churches, which are a strong positive force in these communities.

Using an e-health computer program, half the churches encourage self-regulation by calling people on their cell phones regularly during the day with reminders about exercise and diet. The other half provide informational pamphlets and cancer screenings. These "nudges" toward better health practices, combined with less easy access to unhealthy food and drink, address the issues at both the personal and community levels. It will be exciting to see the outcome of this community-oriented approach and how it might inform future attempts to help people improve their health habits. If successful, it suggests a way that trusted networks might help increase temperate behaviors in larger populations.

## SELF-REGULATION AND NEUROSCIENCE: THE BRAIN IS MORE FLEXIBLE THAN WE REALIZED

Scientists are learning more and more about the nerve processes that underlie how we learn to control our behavior in response to our environment. Psychologists Janet Metcalfe and Walter Mischel suggest that there are two kinds of neural processing. The "hot" process entails making quick, emotional decisions through memory that is based in the brain's amygdala. The "cool" process is slower, more "knowing," and involves the hippocampus and frontal lobes. The cool system develops later and becomes more active as people age, perhaps accounting, in part, for the impulsive, "hot" poor judgment we see in adolescents and the increasing prudence and conscientiousness seen at older ages as the cool process develops.

Many of us were brought up to believe that the brain was the only organ that didn't change after maturity. But it turns out that isn't true. Some very exciting research has shown us that the relationship between our brains and our behavior is a two-way street; the brain directs behavior, but behavior also affects the brain. Building on the work of endocrinologist Hans Selye and physiologist Walter Cannon, neuroscientist Bruce McEwen and his colleagues studied how our life experiences affect our brain function and vice versa. As in life, where we are always striking a balance between too little and too much (whether it is moderation in food, drink, work, or play), the body also strives for balance among its biological systems, three in particular:

the autonomic nervous system, which includes such processes as heart rate, digestion, and breathing, among others;

the metabolic and immune systems, which are responsible for stability and resistance to diseases; and

the hypothalamic/pituitary/adrenal axis of the endocrine system, which helps in regulating the body and managing our reactions to stress.

This kind of biological balance is called homeostasis. When we encounter a stress or trauma, this balance is tipped. For example, if we're taking a pleasant walk in the country and, suddenly, out of the corner of one eye, we spy a grizzly bear that is too close for comfort, we experience fear, which kicks a number of systems into gear. Cortisol, the key hormone released in response to stress, activates the autonomic nervous system, even before we're consciously aware of it, for instance, through changes in our breathing, heart rate, and blood pressure. This system prepares us for the increased energy necessary for our "fight-or-flight" response to danger.

Once we're safely out of harm's way, the body returns to normal, or homeostasis. McEwen refers to this aspect of brain function as allostasis, which is depicted in Figure 10.3. The allostatic response is designed to return the body to normal as quickly as possible. There are many kinds of responses to stress in addition to fight or flight, including personal behaviors like smoking, changes in diet, and exercise. Our genetics and prior experiences also impact how we respond to stress, not to mention humor, which, you may remember, is associated with lower levels of cortisol in our systems.

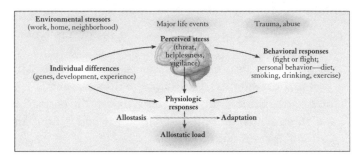

**Figure 10.3**  McEwen's allostatic load model

From Protective and damaging effects of stress mediators, McEwen, B. S., *New England Journal of Medicine*, Jan 15, Vol. 338 (3), pp. 171–179. Copyright 1998 Massachusetts Medical Society. Reprinted with permission from Massachusetts Medical Society.

McEwen points out that not all stressors are bad for us in the long run. Some stress is actually good and is experienced as a challenge to be mastered. After a challenge has been met successfully, the person feels an enhanced sense of mastery, self-esteem, and resilience, which bodes well for meeting the next stress. The accumulation of these kinds of experiences over a lifetime helps to teach us resilience in older age and enhances our sense of personal courage.

But what happens when the stresses are chronic? When a person experiences stress that is prolonged or chronic or occurs in the context of chronic chaos, abuse, or neglect, the system can't quite get back to normal; it remains in the "on" position, so to speak, causing wear and tear on the body's systems. This constant "on" state—called allostatic load—can cause a range of problems from suppressed immune functioning, to bone loss, to poorer concentration and memory. When McEwen and his colleagues looked at the brains of people with a high allostatic load, they found changes in various areas including neurons that had shorter dendrites and fewer synaptic connections. This meant that the nerve cells had fewer connections to each other.

Fortunately, the brain's plasticity works both ways. And we also know how dynamic an organ it is. If the environment can cause negative brain changes, it can also cause positive ones, even into adulthood and older age. Neuroimaging studies show, for example, that brisk exercise can improve cognitive function, resulting in more gray matter in the prefrontal cortex (important for decision-making and moderating social behavior), temporal cortex (important for memory, language, and emotion), and the hippocampus (particularly important for memory). Epidemiologist Michele Carlson and colleagues found that elders who volunteered to work with children for Experience Corps showed better cognitive functioning after six months and that their functional magnetic resonance imaging showed increased activity in their prefrontal cortex (which controls higher mental function).

## BEHAVIOR, SELF-CONTROL, AND THE IMPORTANCE OF ATTITUDES ABOUT AGING

Attitude is one of the ways we can develop healthier habits, even if they don't come to us naturally. In particular, this applies to our attitudes toward aging, even when we're young. In a series of longitudinal studies of elders, Becca Levy's group at Yale found that attitudes about aging could impact our health and even mortality (Levy et al., 2002, 2004, 2009, 2011). One study looked at 600 adults between the ages of 50 and 94, using a scale to measure self-perceptions of aging, with statements like, "Things keep getting worse" and "As you get older, you get more useless." When these people were followed up—some for as long as 23 years—those who had started with a positive self-perception of aging lived seven and a half years longer than whose with a negative self-perception (Figure 10.4).

In another study, the group looked at the attitudes toward aging of hundreds of healthy adults under the age of 49 with no evidence of heart disease. When those subjects were followed up thirty years later, those who'd had negative stereotypes about aging when younger went on to have significantly more heart problems over the next thirty years than those who'd had positive views of aging.

Similar to McEwen's concept of allostatic load, these kinds of studies suggest that the burden of fearing or anticipating aging has a negative effect. How might this attitude affect illness? One likely explanation is that people with a more positive attitude are more likely to attend more to overall healthy habits such as eating a balanced diet, exercising more, drinking less alcohol, being less likely to smoke,

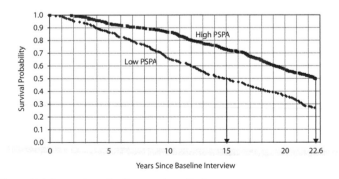

**Figure 10.4** Longevity and self-perceptions of aging

Reproduced from Levy, B. R., Slade, M. D., Kunkel, S. R., & Kasl, S. V. (2002). Longevity increased by positive self-perceptions of aging. *J Pers Soc Psychol, 83*(2), p. 264. Reprinted with permission from American Psychological Association.

and having more regular health examinations. While no explanation has been proven, temperance makes good sense if you're looking forward to a good life in your later years.

Does this mean that if we do get sick, it's our own fault, as the nineteenth century health reformers believed? Of course not. These data are very general, and we are all vulnerable to the vagaries of unexpected illnesses that come on without rhyme or reason, regardless of our personal behavior. But it is useful to know how helpful it can potentially be to cultivate a realistic, positive attitude toward aging, even when we're younger.

The sense of positive self-control and self-efficacy can also affect memory. In one large long-term study by the Levy group, people who had started out with more positive attitudes toward aging performed significantly better on memory tasks thirty-eight years later (Figure 10.5). The mechanism for this process is not yet known. One possibility is that having a positive view of aging goes hand in hand with maintaining a more active and interactive lifestyle, which may help to maintain memory longer.

## SELF-REGULATION AND A SENSE OF PURPOSE

Similar to Levy's work, Patricia Boyle and her colleagues at Rush Medical Center studied elders' cognitive function in relation to their sense of having a purpose in life, over a number of years. Subjects were asked whether they felt there was some meaning in their experiences and whether they had pursued worthwhile goals. At the same time, Boyle and colleagues measured their cognitive functioning in areas such as memory. After the subjects' deaths,

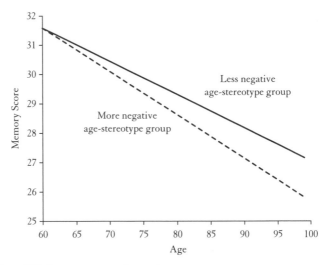

**Figure 10.5** Age stereotypes and memory

Levy, BR, Zonderman, AB, Slade, MD, & Ferrucci, L. (2011). Memory shaped by age stereotypes over time. Journals of Gerontology, Series B: Psychological Sciences and Social Sciences, 67(4), p. 434. Reprinted by permission of Oxford University Press.

autopsies were performed to confirm the presence and extent of Alzheimer's disease.

The experimenters found that the people who felt a greater sense of purpose also performed better on cognitive tasks, even when their brains showed an equal burden of disease. Over seven years, a person with a high score on purpose was more than twice as likely to remain free of the symptoms of Alzheimer's disease than those with lower scores. These data can't tell us whether the sense of purpose led to less Alzheimer's illness or whether the people with less illness were better able to pursue goals and have a stronger sense of purpose. Hopefully, future research will help sort out more of this fascinating relationship.

## BACK TO REAL LIFE: FINDING A WAY TO ADAPT

Because we have the ability to moderate and control aspects of our behavior, we continue to adapt and change as we seek the right balance among our health needs, desires, and limitations, whether physical or psychological.

### Emily: Self-Control and Knowing Yourself

Emily, in her late 40s, recently experienced a series of medical problems. She'd had multiple surgeries over the previous three years for a combination of problems involving her breathing and vocal chords. It was a very difficult time, as she never knew if there would be a new complication requiring yet another surgery. She wanted to lose some of the weight she'd accumulated over the years, but she found it difficult to exercise, especially since she hated it so much.

Finally, after three years, the complications ended, and the final surgery was a success. Grateful to have her life back after her ordeal, she found new energy, some of which she wanted to devote to getting her body back on track. So, she discovered that although she hated gym machines, she loved the swimming pool and weights, too. She found a balance by skipping the exercises she hated and focusing on the ones she loved.

"I've now lost 32 pounds," Emily triumphantly reports, "and I have muscles in my arms and legs! So cool. Plus, I have tons of energy! And focus with it."

And it is not impossible for elders to remain in remarkably good physical and mental health. In February 2013, 101-year-old Fauja Singh finished a marathon in Hong Kong, his ninth in the past decade. Called the "Turbaned Tornado," he says he started running after the tragic loss of his son. He found solace "because of the happiness I get from it. If something makes you happy you'll do it well." Famous swimmer Diana Nyad finally succeeded in her goal of being the first person to swim from Cuba to Florida without a shark cage. She did this at the age of 64, after 35 years of trying. In other words, she succeeded in doing at age 64 what she couldn't accomplish when she was 29.

## GETTING HELP TO IMPROVE SELF-CONTROL AND AVOID EXCESS

Sometimes, people can simply make a decision to change their behavior and just do it cold turkey. But it's very common for us to need help, as our problematic behaviors can take on a life of their own, whether or not the medical community considers them to be physical addictions or diseases.

### Joe: Help in Finding a New Approach

Joe was a 65-year-old businessman who came in to see Jimmie for help in managing his obesity while he was being treated for prostate cancer. He had also suffered a hip fracture, which caused a permanent limp, and he walked with a cane. Fortunately, his job didn't require much physical exertion, but he was stymied in his efforts to deal with his weight.

Joe described a not uncommon up-and-down pattern of weight loss and gain—overeating, gaining weight, and then exercising and losing it. But, now, exercise was no longer possible. The only way he could lose weight this time would be to control his diet, which he just couldn't seem to do.

Joe began to work with a psychologist whom Jimmie recommended who guided, goaded, and supported him in following a healthy but rigorous diet over several months. At the six-month mark, Joe proudly told Jimmie how he had lost forty pounds! "I have a new life now," he said. "I can walk more easily, have fewer pains, and I feel so much better about myself." Joe exuded a new level of confidence. The psychological burden of not feeling in control of his body was replaced by a sense of pride and a feeling of self-efficacy.

How do we learn to manage those behaviors that are fine in moderation but destructive in excess? For example, alcohol, which is available to adults, could not successfully be legislated out of our society. Criminalizing marijuana and recreational drugs has not stopped their use, either.

Clearly, many people can handle alcohol or risky behaviors without excessive use or addiction. But one person's friendly weekly poker game can, for someone else, spiral into a compulsive gambling habit. In general, treatments have not been impressively successful, but some have proved very helpful for many people.

The most famous of these programs was started by Bill Wilson. A severe alcoholic, he had a religious awakening that led him to stop drinking in 1935. He began to help other alcoholics and found that helping them also helped him to stay sober. He was soon joined by a physician, Dr. Bob. Together, they began to contact others, and within a year or so, they had helped more than 100 people fight the urge to drink. They created Alcoholics Anonymous, which had a spiritual component in that alcoholics were encouraged to give themselves over to a higher power. How each person defined that higher power was up to him or her. Psychiatrist Arnold Ludwig encountered one person who even prayed to "To Whom it May Concern."

Paradoxically, Bill W. and Dr. Bob sought to improve their level of self-control by ceding some of that control to a higher power, making failures more tolerable and putting less pressure on themselves. The virtue of humility was being called upon to help gain perspective. While not for everyone, AA has been an indispensable part of many people's recovery. Nothing else had worked for Dorothy, whom we mentioned in chapter 5, until she found AA. And, like Bill W., a very key part of her continued recovery was helping other women who were in similar situations, which helped her transcend her own limitations.

One aspect of AA's program is to learn to recognize "stinkin' thinkin'," or patterns and attitudes that might bring one closer to falling off the wagon. Other programs, like G. Alan Marlatt's Relapse Prevention Program, particularly focus on learning to control behaviors by being aware of how our environment might cue us to behave in certain ways and/or forms of thinking that might lead us into dangerous territory.

One such way of thinking is "apparently irrelevant decisions," or AIDs, which lead us into tempting situations. For example, one day, a few months after Marlatt himself had quit smoking, he "innocently" found himself sitting in the smoking section of an airplane. As he smelled the cigarettes all around him, he couldn't fight the strong impulse to smoke. Next time, he made a conscious effort to reserve a seat far away from the smoking section.

Regardless of the particular problem with moderation, all these programs have a few things in common. First, they involve recognizing the limits to what we can and can't control; they also involve compensation by controlling our environment or finding tolerable alternatives. They do this in a supportive atmosphere, rather than a judgmental one. And they suggest concrete steps to take in the context of a community that understands how hard it is to take them. Moderation is easier to practice in the context of like-minded people.

Whether we exercise them in a group or alone, moderation and self-control help us enjoy our lives. The earlier we start, the longer we can reap their benefits and hand over a healthier body to our older selves. But even if we don't start at a young age, thanks to the brain's plasticity and our ability to find new ways to do the things that are good for us, we can still reap their benefits for years to come. (But, of course, that doesn't mean we can't enjoy a nice piece of chocolate sometimes!)

## REFERENCES

Alcoholics Anonymous. (1955). *Alcoholics Anonymous:Tthe Story of How Many Thousands of Men and Women Have Recovered from Alcoholism.* New York: Alcoholics Anonymous Publishing, Inc.

Allemand, M., Steiner, M., and Hill, P. L. (2013). Effects of a forgiveness intervention for older adults. *J Couns Psychol, 60*(2), 279–286.

Alvarez, L. (2013, September 3, 2013). Sharks absent, swimmer, 64, strokes from Cuba to Florida. *New York Times*, p. A1.

Baumeister, R. F., Heatherton, T. F., and Tice, D. M. (1994). *Losing Control: How and Why People Fail at Self-Regulation.* San Diego: Academic Press.

Boyle, P. A., Buchman, A. S., Barnes, L. L., and Bennett, D. A. (2010). Effect of a purpose in life on risk of incident Alzheimer disease and mild cognitive impairment in community-dwelling older persons. *Arch Gen Psychiatry, 67*(3), 304–310.

Boyle, P. A., Buchman, A. S., Wilson, R. S., Yu, L., Schneider, J. A., and Bennett, D. A. (2012). Effect of purpose in life on the relation between Alzheimer disease pathologic changes on cognitive function in advanced age. *Arch Gen Psychiatry, 69*(5), 499–505.

Butler, R. N. (2008). *The Longevity Revolution: The Benefits and Challenges of Living a Long Life.* New York: Perseus.

Carlson, M. C., Erickson, K. I., Kramer, A. F., Voss, M. W., Bolea, N., Mielke, M., McGill, S., Rebok, G. W., Seeman, T., and Fried, L. P. (2009). Evidence for neurocognitive plasticity in at-risk older adults: The Experience Corps program. *J Gerontol A Biol Sci Med Sci, 64*(12), 1275–1282.

Carstensen, L. L., Pasupathi, M., Mayr, U., and Nesselroade, J. R. (2000). Emotional experience in everyday life across the adult life span. *J Pers Soc Psychol, 79*(4), 644–655.

Cicero, M. T. *Treatises on Friendships and Old Age.* (44 BC). from http://www.gutenberg.org/ebooks/2808

Cole, S. W., Hawkley, L. C., Arevalo, J. M., Sung, C. Y., Rose, R. M., and Cacioppo, J. T. (2007). Social regulation of gene expression in human leukocytes. *Genome Biol, 8*(9), R189.

Danese, A., and McEwen, B. S. (2012). Adverse childhood experiences, allostasis, allostatic load, and age-related disease. *Physiol Behav, 106*(1), 29–39.

Erikson, E. H. (1950). *Childhood and Society.* New York: Norton.

Hunt, K. (2013, February 25, 2013). "Turbaned tornado," world's oldest marathon runner, retires. *CNN.com.*

Kaufman, M. T. (1995, February 22, 1995). Old man with a horn: Still swinging. *The New York Times.*

Levy, B. R., Slade, M. D., Kunkel, S. R., and Kasl, S. V. (2002). Longevity increased by positive self-perceptions of aging. *J Pers Soc Psychol*, *83*(2), 261–270.

Levy, B. R., and Myers, L. M. (2004). Preventive health behaviors influenced by self-perceptions of aging. *Prev Med*, *39*(3), 625–629.

Levy, B. R., Zonderman, A. B., Slade, M. D., and Ferrucci, L. (2009). Age stereotypes held earlier in life predict cardiovascular events in later life. *Psychol Sci*, *20*(3), 296–298.

Levy, B. R., Zonderman, A. B., Slade, M. D., and Ferrucci, L. (2011). Memory shaped by age stereotypes over time. *J Gerontol B Psychol Sci Soc Sci*, *67*(4), 432–436.

Low, C. A., Matthews, K. A., and Hall, M. (2013). Elevated C-reactive protein in adolescents: roles of stress and coping. *Psychosom Med, 75*(5), 449–452.

Ludwig, A. M. (1988). *Understanding the Alcoholic's Mind: The Nature of Craving and How to Control It*. New York: Oxford University Press.

Magai, C., and Halpern, B. (2001). Emotional development during the middle years. In M. E. Lachman (ed.), *Handbook of Midlife Development* (pp. 310–344). New York: Wiley.

Marlatt, G. A., and Donovan, D. M. (Eds.) (2005). *Relapse Prevention: Maintenance Strategies in the Treatment of Addictive Behaviors*. New York: Guilford.

May, W. (1986). The virtues and vices of the elderly. In T. R. Cole and S. A. Gadow (eds.), *What Does It Mean to Grow Old: Reflections from the Humanities* (pp. 61–77). Durham, NC: Duke University Press.

McEwen, B.S. (2006). Protective and damaging effects of stress mediators. *New England Journal of Medicine*, Jan 15, Vol. *338* (3), pp. 171–179.

McEwen, B. S., and Gianaros, P. J. (2011). Stress- and allostasis-induced brain plasticity. *Annu Rev Med*, *62*, 431–445.

Metcalfe, J., and Mischel, W. (1999). A hot/cool-system analysis of delay of gratification: Dynamics of willpower. *Psychol Rev, 106*(1), 3–19.

Mischel, W., Shoda, Y., and Peake, P. K. (1988). The nature of adolescent competencies predicted by preschool delay of gratification. *J Pers Soc Psychol*, *54*(4), 687–696.

Moffitt, T. E., Arseneault, L., Belsky, D., Dickson, N., Hancox, R. J., Harrington, H., Houts, R., Poulton, R., Roberts, B. W., Ross, S., Sears, M. R., Thomson, W. M., and Caspi, A. (2011). A gradient of childhood self-control predicts health, wealth, and public safety. *Proc Natl Acad Sci U S A*, *108*(7), 2693–2698.

Peterson, C., and Seligman, M. E. P. (2004). Universal virtues?—Lessons from history. In C. Peterson and M. E. P. Seligman, eds., *Character Strengths and Virtues*. New York: Oxford University Press, 33–51.

Sacks, O. (2013). The joy of old age (no kidding). *The New York Times*, p. SR12.

Schroeder, S. A. (2007). Shattuck lecture. We can do better—Improving the health of the American people. *N Engl J Med*, *357*(12), 1221–1228.

Stengel, R. (2009). *Mandela's Way*. New York: Crown Archetype.

Stringhini, S., Berkman, L., Dugravot, A., Ferrie, J. E., Marmot, M., Kivimaki, M., and Singh-Manoux, A. (2012). Socioeconomic status, structural and functional measures of social support, and mortality: The British Whitehall II Cohort Study, 1985–2009. *Am J Epidemiol*, *175*(12), 1275–1283.

Tzu, L. (1999). *Tao Te Ching: An Illustrated Journey*. S. Mitchell, trans. New York: Harper Collins.

# 11

# The Virtue of Passing on to the Next Generation

## The Bridge Between Past and Future

*If I'd known how wonderful grandchildren were,*
*I would have had them first.*

### Lachlan and Gramps

A colleague, James Strain, tells the story of a trip to Mozambique he took with his wife and their 7-year-old grandson, Lachlan. They were on Tofu Beach, where they had the opportunity to join a scientist on a launch survey and swim with whale sharks, the largest fish in existence. Their boat came alongside some whale sharks that were 60 feet long. The scientist called out to the Strains to jump in and swim, but Lachlan hesitated. "But, Gramps, they're too big to swim with. They can hurt me." Jim quickly reassured him, "If you just touch them with your finger, they'll dive and leave you alone. It isn't how big something is that's important, it is how you feel about it."

At school soon after, two bullies tried to push Lachlan around. He found the courage to say, "You may be bigger, but I can get you into trouble!" It turned out that Gramps's lesson about whale sharks was also a lesson about bullying. Sometimes, the perspective of the older generation can truly change the landscape for a younger person.

Just as the experience of having a young protégé can change the life of the elder for the better, it also works in the reverse. The grandparent–grandchild relationship is a particularly poignant and meaningful version of that relationship. In fact, Jimmie has a test for determining when an older person is truly depressed. She calls it the Grandma Test.

After Jimmie asks how an elder has been doing in general, if she is a grandparent, Jimmie says, "Well, tell me about your grandkids." The usual response is a wide, joyful smile. But if the smile doesn't come or if the response is, "I can't even enjoy my grandchildren anymore," Jimmie knows there is trouble that needs attention. Talking about grandchildren brings out such joy that, sometimes, the talker doesn't notice that the listener has heard enough. Jimmie recalls one woman who, as a resident of an assisted living center, was so annoyed by the "grandchild competition contest" each day that she invented a set of grandchildren just to keep up.

There's an old joke that the reason that grandparents and grandchildren love each other so much is that they have a common enemy. In fact, as we saw in chapter 2, they might have a bit more in common than that, as well. Both might be more likely to enjoy *living lighter* and be better able to appreciate each other without all the baggage of responsibility that weighs down the generation between them. The members of the Vintage Readers Book Club suggest that it's the lightness that allows elder and younger to share a greater freedom to laugh.

And we should point out that this relationship works both ways. There's a lot that grandparents learn from their grandchildren, as well. This is particularly true when it comes to technology, which recently has been developing at a faster pace than ever before.

## THE JOY OF LEARNING FROM THE YOUNG

Jimmie's introduction to e-mail came about fifteen years ago when she received her first e-mail message from her granddaughter. It became clear that if she wanted to communicate the modern way, Jimmie had better learn from her granddaughter how to do it. Now, the communication has switched to even more instantaneous texting, and even e-mail is too slow for teenagers. So, the learning curve continues. Teenagers readily learn to use these new communication devices, and many elders continue to be terribly awkward with each new iteration of these "infernal" machines (to use a phrase appreciated by elders). Grandchildren enjoy the reversed role of being teacher, as elders humbly are taught by them to use unfamiliar technology.

### Grandma Software

Jimmie's 8-year-old grandson, Daniel, has taken things another step. With an entrepreneurial bent, he sent her the following e-mail about the new company he'd created:

Subject: The Grandma Software: Making Being a Grandma Way Easier

Dear Jimmie Holland,

We, at 31M have put out a new software called the Grandma Software. In this software you have a screen and when you need something, you tap and someone comes to help you. It is designed for Hollands that are 65–90 years old, and we are wondering if you would like one. If you would, send us a letter or e-mail us.

Needless to say, Jimmie is a proud owner of the Grandma Software! Dragged into the computer world kicking and screaming, but guided with such loving young hands, how could she complain? In fact, she now owns Grandma Software 2.0! Jimmie and her husband are the luckiest of grandparents, with marvelous grandchildren who keep them in touch with new ideas—and they cherish their source. Clearly, the most precious gift from grandchildren is the pure joy of sharing in their serious and fun moments (not to mention the fact that elders can give them back to their parents at the end of a tiring day).

It's a good thing that this experience can be so joyful, since grandmothers continue to play a key role in many families as surrogate caregivers for their grandchildren while the parents work. Many grandfathers who are retired also participate. However, grandmothers lead in numbers, representing 43% of all women caregivers. It appears that these women may not only be helpful but might also be increasing the health of their grandchildren.

## THE GRANDMOTHER HYPOTHESIS

Mary Catherine Bateson (2010) describes how studies of species that live in groups—for example, deer—show that the young are more likely to survive if there are a few old does living with the herd. There is a similar body of research related to grandmothers and grandchildren, known as the grandmother hypothesis, put forth by anthropologist Kristen Hawkes and her group (2003). Hawkes suggests that in hunter–gatherer societies of old, grandmothers collected food for the grandchildren and tended the young, which freed their daughters to have more children more quickly and increased the survival chances of the children.

This is no less true today, when working mothers often turn to grandmothers to help in a pinch. Mindy was fortunate to live near both her mother and mother-in-law when her children were little. Needless to say, they were both on speed dial, and both of her children's lives (and her own) were enriched as a result!

Jared Diamond, in his book *The World Until Yesterday*, sums up his many studies of traditional societies and describes their attitudes toward the elders. He points out that older men in those societies who could no longer wield a spear could still hunt smaller animals and make tools. Elder men and women were often the most skilled basketmakers and potters. Most important, in societies with no written language, it was the elders who had the most crucial cultural and survival information: the songs and myths; knowledge of the best grazing grounds and of how previous generations survived during droughts; which plants healed and which killed; the moral lessons learned over centuries of hardships. It was the elders who were usually the priests, medicine men, and leaders.

At a practical level, the older women in the Hadza hunter–gatherer society of Tanzania were among their hardest workers, foraging for tubers and fruit for up to 7 hours a day. In fact, the number of hours they worked was directly correlated with how much weight their grandchildren gained. Diamond (2012) notes a similar situation for eighteenth and nineteenth century Finnish and Canadian farmers. In those cultures, more children survived to adulthood if they had a living grandmother than those who didn't.

While it appears that elders have maintained a useful role in many societies, we can't paint too rosy a picture across the board. In particular, the subject of elder abandonment is a painful and complex one. The custom appears to depend largely on whether elders were deemed a risk to the group's safety. In nomadic societies, which moved all their goods by carrying them, the weak or old were too much of an added burden. And, in some climates where food was scarce for long periods, as in the Arctic, those deemed less able to contribute, such as the elderly, were the last to be fed. In such cases, elders' needs were sacrificed for the sake of the group's survival.

Still, in many of those societies, elders were recognized to have important contributions: grandmothers helped cultivate socially desirable traits in their grandchildren, like cooperation, bonding, and learning new skills. This "grandmother effect" is also believed to have helped our brains grow bigger throughout the course of evolution. As humans started living longer, each stage of life started lasting longer. Children stayed children longer, thereby allowing more time for their brains to develop in more neurologically complex ways. The number of children raised by their grandparents grew to almost 3 million in 2011.

We mentioned the old saying that grandparents and grandchildren have such a great bond because they both have a common enemy. Sandwichers live with a lot of anxiety, not least of which is about doing right by their children. And part of that anxiety stems from the fact that parents won't know until their children reach adulthood just how good a job they did. In the meantime, sandwichers are the ones who are up in the middle of the night when there are nightmares or illnesses and the ones who figure out, on a daily basis, how to balance professional lives, parenting responsibilities, and responsibilities to themselves. What a treat for children when they have these other grownups who can just love them without all that baggage! And what an even greater treat when the relationship bears fruit for everyone, as it did in the case of Jimmie and Madeline, not to mention all the grateful members of the Vintage Readers Books Club.

This intergenerational relationship isn't only for people related by blood. Many of life's most rewarding friendships are those between younger and older generations, which grow out of mentoring experiences or from sharing work, projects, and collaborations. This book grew out of just such a setting and has enriched both our lives. Jimmie recalls three teachers, none of whom had children, who took her under their wing at different times in her life to teach her. But more important, their affection and confidence in her gave her the strength to seek the goals that she aspired to, including becoming a doctor—not the most likely career for a girl who grew up in rural Depression-era Texas.

Jimmie feels the incredible joy of collaborating with the generation that will be taking her place. Mindy, in particular, feels the same about Jimmie's impact on their field, in general, and on her both personally and professionally. Our Wednesday morning meeting to discuss the finer (and not-so-finer) points of aging, sometimes attended by our colleague, Kate, is the high point of the week!

## WHAT DO YOU WISH YOU'D ASKED YOUR GRANDPARENTS WHEN YOU HAD THE CHANCE?

So what do—or should—elders pass on? The older generation has the unique opportunity—and sacred responsibility—to serve as the bridge between the past and the future. The reason that deer herds with elder does survive better is because those deer are better positioned to remember where to find food during droughts or heavy snows. Similarly, older people can talk with eyewitness authenticity about the past, making history come alive for the young. And they can talk about the issues and debates at a particular time in history. The lessons learned are often as relevant to the present as to the prior era. Sometimes to hilarious effect.

A friend of Jimmie's told her about the time her 6-year-old daughter asked, "Mom, were you alive during the war?" Assuming her daughter was asking about World War II, the most recent war at the time, the mother replied, "Of course." "Well," the little girl said, "what did George Washington look like?"

These casual conversations spark the opportunity to explore further and to talk about special family members whom they have never known and about whom they can only learn from someone who shared the lives of those now gone. It is a time to share stories about their special qualities—virtues like courage and social justice—using old pictures of places that give the young a sense of where they came from. Sharon, a woman in her 60s, shared memories and photographs of her grandparents with her niece, who'd never met them. Her niece was amazed at some of the similarities between her and family members she'd never met, like personality quirks and musical talents.

We often miss opportunities for these kinds of discussions with elders and then find it is too late, and the information is gone forever. How many times have you heard, "I wish I had asked Grandpa about. . . ?" The stories are there and the elders enjoy telling stories from the past. The more we set up situations and encourage cross-generational conversations, the better.

One big down side of assisted living is that it reduces the daily opportunity for interaction between old and young in a comfortable, casual setting. A particularly successful example of this kind of opportunity, described earlier, is Experience Corps, the organization sponsored by AARP that encourages elders from the community to volunteer in local inner-city schools.

The Experience Corps provides an experience that simulates grandparenting for both generations. As we mentioned, both students and elders (mostly women participate) report benefits; the children have a chance for extra tutoring, and early research suggests they are less likely to be sent to the principal's office and more likely to read better. As one mother wrote, "We're trying to get in touch with the [Experience Corps] tutor because we want to invite her to Cassie's First Communion. She has to be there. She's the one who made Cassie love to read!"

At the same time, the elders feel like they're doing something meaningful and useful. The recent study by Boyle and colleagues (described in chapter 10) shows that the benefits are not only psychological; elders with a greater sense of purpose and meaning maintained better cognitive skills. Another study we mentioned, by epidemiologist Michelle Carlson and colleagues (2009), showed that elders got even more direct cognitive benefits from the program, particularly in complex decision-making and other activities, even though they were a population at risk for cognitive loss, not gain. These kinds of findings tell us that mental activity combined with a sense of doing something meaningful for others is a win–win proposition for mental and physical health.

The good news is that there are ways for people in different generations to keep connected in meaningful ways. Today's cadre of home health aides includes remarkably sensitive and caring women who become surrogate daughters and granddaughters, with the teaching and learning often going in both directions.

## Bella and Anna

Bella Friedman is a 92-year-old retired librarian who never married and whose family and close friends have passed away. She enjoyed photography and water color painting in her retirement, but a tremor and neck pain began to interfere with these pleasures as well as daily chores. Bella began to fear that she wouldn't be able to stay in her apartment, but the idea of moving to assisted living was wholly unappealing. We suggested that she have someone come in to help her. She found Anna, a woman from South Africa, who helped with chores and shopping and carried the camera so that Bella could start taking pictures again.

As Anna became Bella's valued companion, Bella began to teach her facts about the United States and to help her with her immigration status. She proudly talked about how bright and smart Anna was, sounding as delighted as if she were describing her own daughter.

## WHAT ARE SOME WAYS OF PASSING THINGS ON?

Food is a central part of family life, and Jimmie loves the fact that her children love the Texas fried chicken that she makes exactly like her mother and grandmother did. Many of the most important discussions between generations are likely to occur around the kitchen table. The coffee comes out with dessert, the dishes are put away, and there is a sense of safety and comfort in the intimate conversations that would not likely happen in more formal circumstances. Sharing food somehow encourages sharing ideas, and often the most important issues come up in that context. Jimmie has kept a sampler in her kitchen for more than fifty years:

*Life's riches other rooms adorn,*
*But in a kitchen home is born.*

When her daughters complained that her recipes looked like a mess in the kitchen—note cards smudged with butter and chocolate—they insisted she put them into a book. So, she did. She realized that this was an opportunity to collect not only the recipes but also to describe the people who had contributed them over the years. Now, every recipe includes the year of its acquisition and something about the person that made her memorable to Jimmie. Now, they could all be "remembered" by others, too. And at holidays, Jimmie fields queries about recipes, so her family can be sure they are doing it right.

We are often unaware—or uninformed—about the generations that came before, those who may have made their mark on us without our ever realizing it. Photos are also helpful. Jimmie keeps a section of a wall for her own and her husband's family photos, which are the source of stories from the past.

Written stories also keep the past alive. Jimmie and two of her Texas friends put together the stories of their mothers' lives in the 1930s. Before electricity came to rural areas, life was far more difficult: well water pulled up and heated for cooking and baths; an ice box for refrigeration; kerosene lamps; an outhouse; vegetables pulled from the garden; laundry and ironing done by hand; the chicken for Sunday dinner killed in the chicken yard in the early morning. Preparation for family holidays took days of baking and cooking. How they got other things done is quite remarkable, and yet they nurtured their children and managed their homes with minimal help from the men, whose role was clearly defined as belonging outside the home.

Jimmie loved to listen to her mother and her aunt talk and laugh about the old days and their own foibles. She recorded many of those lively conversations, which make for a wonderful account of the family history for the grandchildren.

## HOW WE SEE OURSELVES AND OUR
## PARENTS

One interesting aspect of aging is how our views of our-selves and our parents change over time. When we're young, the idea that we might be similar to our parents is just unthinkable. Thirty-somethings often come to think, "I can't believe how much smarter my parents are now than when I was growing up." We really don't begin to appreciate our parents as simply people until we reach a certain level of personal maturity. As we get older, we're more likely to find ourselves using a familiar expression and suddenly thinking, "That sounded just like my father!" Or recognizing voice qualities or unique expressions and even facial features that seem to cross generations.

We smile when we think about our parents' virtues—and the valuable lessons we're grateful for their having taught us. As years go by, we find ourselves dwelling less on their vices. Part of reaching maturity as adults is that we become more willing—and able—to forgive and forget or at least let go of our parents' mistakes. Just as we hope our own children will do for us down the line.

### Linda Moore: Looking Ahead

Almost 60, with her father in particularly failing health, Linda is aware of the things she's learning from her parents, both positive and negative. "My father has done a remarkable job of making peace with his life," she says. "He ponders things, and can get himself really down, though he does have a great sense of humor. My mother doesn't ponder things in a deep or anxious way. She's realistic and practical." "I'm a more pondering sort, like my father," Linda confesses, "so, I know I have to make an effort to 'smell the flowers'. I've learned tools from them for making peace, later on."

Perhaps equally important in terms of passing on is not just facts and stories but what is less tangible and much harder to identify—our sense of values and personal philosophies of what constitutes living a good life. Certainly it is one thing to espouse high moral values, but we well know that this has a lot less impact on our kids compared with how they see us act and who we are. Bateson (2010) wrote thoughtfully about the process and its limitations:

> *We cannot instruct our children to trust, but we can try to be trustworthy and we can make a practice of showing trust in them. We can teach love by loving and will by consistency. We can make them more beautiful by responding to their beauty. We can give then hope and courage for their lives by the way we respond to the diminishments of age, or at the last by the manner of our dying.*
>
> And yet, she reminds us, "We cannot fully pass on what we have learned from experience because the living was necessary to the learning" (245).

When Jimmie and her husband, James, took their second son to Bard College, the college president, Leon Botstein, both consoled and warned the departing parents: "Your children will turn out to be more like you than you ever hoped—or feared."

It requires a great deal of patience and faith to believe that our children will grow into good citizens; that they will have the confidence that comes from knowing they're somebody important in the world and the humility that comes from knowing that so is everyone else. Indeed, Jimmie's children have grown up with the values their parents had always hoped they would embrace. They are loving parents and responsible citizens of the world. They have grown their own mighty oaks, which their parents admire from a distance—and bask in their shade at times. Jimmie sees how her mother's motto, "You must help to make the world a little better place," is being passed on, and she couldn't be prouder. Mindy looks forward to being able to say the same of her two boys one day.

Being a bridge between the past and future requires a transcendent willingness to think and plan beyond our finite lives, what Erik Erikson (1950) referred to as our widening social radius. But it also suggests a recognition of the finiteness of life and concern for those who will follow and what their world will be like. Concerns for the fate of the planet, for consequences of global warming, for the conflicts that persist, and the wars that continue to break out—they are part of this need—and indeed commitment to the broader future of humanity in general.

One additional thing elders may pass on is simply who they are. They are viewed by the younger with trepidation: "My God, will I be like that someday?" Thinking back, Jimmie can recall elders who had qualities that she admired—and still admires—in her memories. They have served her as models of values that she has tried to emulate.

And Mindy admires Jimmie and other elders for serving as her model, which she hopes to emulate, too.

The writer Judith Viorst (2000) captures in poetry the emotions that are hard to express about subjects dear to our hearts. This poem from *Suddenly Sixty* encompasses the wishes for the people we love—and those we will likely never see.

**The Sweetest of Nights and the Finest of Days:**

**A Song for Our Children and Our Children's Children**[*]

I wish you, I wish you,

I wish you these wishes:

Cool drinks in your glasses,

Warm food in your dishes.

People to nourish and cherish and love you.

A lamp in the window to light your way home in the haze.

I wish you the sweetest of night

And the finest of days.

I wish, I wish you

A talent for living.

Delight in the getting,

Delight in the giving.

A song in your soul and someone to hear it.

---

The wisdom to find the right path

when you're lost in a maze.

I wish you the sweetest of nights

And the finest of days.

A snug roof above.

A strong self inside you.

The courage to go where you know you must go.

And a good heart to guide you.

And good friends beside you.

I wish you, I wish you

A dream worth the doing.

And fortune's face smiling

On all you're pursuing.

And pleasures these far far

Outweigh your small sorrows.

Arms opened wide to embrace your tomorrows.

A long sunlit sail on the bluest and smoothest of bays.

I wish you the sweetest of nights

And the finest of days.

## REFERENCES

American Association of Retired Persons. AARP Experience Corps: Stories from families. Retrieved July 10, 2013, from http://www.aarp.org/experience-corps/our-stories/experience-corps-family-stories.html

Bateson, M. C. (2010). *Composing a Further Life: The Age of Active Wisdom*. New York: Alfred A. Knopf.

Carlson, M. C., Erickson, K. I., Kramer, A. F., Voss, M. W., Bolea, N., Mielke, M., McGill, S., Rebok, G. W., Seeman, T., and Fried, L. P. (2009). Evidence for neurocognitive plasticity in at-risk older adults: The Experience Corps program. *J Gerontol A Biol Sci Med Sci*, *64*(12), 1275–1282.

Diamond, J. (2012). *The World Until Yesterday: What Can We Learn from Traditional Societies?* New York: Viking.

Erikson, E. H. (1950). *Childhood and Society*. New York: Norton.

Hawkes, K. (2003). Grandmothers and the evolution of human longevity. *Am J Hum Biol, 15*(3), 380–400.

Magai, C., and Halpern, B. (2001). Emotional development during the middle years. In M. E. Lachman (ed.), *Handbook of Midlife Development* (pp. 310–344): Wiley.

Shulevitz, J. (2013, February 11, 2013). Why do grandmothers exist? Solving an evolutionary mystery. *The New Republic*.

Viorst, J. (2000). The Sweetest of Nights and the Finest of Days: A song for our Children and our Children's Children *Suddenly Sixty and Other Shocks of Later Life* (pp. 60–61). New York: Simon and Schuster.

# Part III

# Putting the Virtues to Work

# 12

# When Older Doesn't Feel Lighter

## Loneliness and Social Isolation

*At 94, I miss having someone to hug and someone to hug me. I am thinking of getting a little dog so I have at least some living thing to cuddle with.*
— Marjorie

As we saw in the last chapter, human beings are social animals who need each other to survive and flourish, at all ages. The sense of calm that comes from simply holding a friend's hand or being given a friendly hug during a moment of crisis tells the whole story. Human contact helps us develop all the virtues we've been discussing, like humanity and concern for our fellow man; courage in the face of hardship or fear; transcendence through sharing joy with another. Other people remind us, literally, of our common humanity and can help us feel like we belong. They even help us laugh.

But the potential for social isolation and loneliness can be a particular problem at older ages. Marjorie, the nonagenarian we quoted above, especially misses the physical contact that comes from having a caring person close by. Even if many elders feel *lighter as they go*, some may feel weighted down with worry or sadness if they don't have enough social support.

## THE CONCRETE IMPACT OF SOCIAL SUPPORT—OR ITS ABSENCE

### *Modern Life and Social Ties*

Social ties were once simpler and more enduring when people lived and died in the same communities and elders were an integral part of the fabric of village life, interacting with all ages. But modern life interrupted that pattern. Now, families are more likely to be scattered across cities, states, and even countries or continents, and there are more and more single-person or small households. The US Census Bureau estimated that 31 million Americans were living alone in 2010, an increase of 40% in thirty years. A large portion of those single-person households are comprised of older people living alone.

While many elders would find more and richer opportunities for social contacts and activities if they moved to retirement communities, most hold on tenaciously to their homes or apartments, even if it means living alone with few daily social contacts. These are the places where they've lived independently most of their lives, having created a comfortable haven from the world. Weighing living alone at home versus moving to an unfamiliar communal assisted living setting—with its built in social environment—is not an easy choice.

Another reason that elders might feel more alone is that their adult daughters are much more likely to be working than in previous generations and have less time to care for their parents. And both adult sons and daughters are more likely to have started families at older ages and are dealing later with career and younger children at the same time.

A related problem is transportation, which becomes more difficult both for adult children (especially if they have young children of their own) and those elders who had been able to visit more easily when younger. Elder peers may be less able to visit each other, especially if they no longer drive or need to use a walker or wheelchair.

Another issue that faces elders the longer they live is the loss of old friends. Like the joke about the woman who's asked what's the best thing about being 104, "No peer pressure," she says. While many elders can manage to make friends despite such losses, most acknowledge that it can be hard to make new friends when you're older.

### Ramona: Alone in a Crowd

Ramona is an 80-year-old woman who grew up with a father who was bright but distant. Intellectual and shy, she had always found it difficult to make friends. Though she found and married a man who adored her, she generally avoided social situations as much as she could. She had one son who, like her father, was bright but distant. Despite misgivings about the strained relationship with her son, Ramona generally fared well through her midlife years; she had a rich intellectual life and a good relationship with her husband.

When Ramona got older, her husband died. She developed severe arthritis and pulmonary fibrosis, which caused her great pain and limited her walking. In order to be able to stay in her home, she needed the help of home health aides. But Ramona was always uncomfortable having other people around and either fired them or criticized them, which drove them away. Reluctantly, she went to an assisted living residence, already convinced that she would not like the place or fit in. She assumed other people would be less intellectual and that they wouldn't have much in common to talk about.

Ramona had a completely different experience than outgoing Maureen Davis, the Honorary Director of her own assisted living residence, whom we described in chapter 5. Staying to herself, Ramona preferred the newspaper to interacting with other elders. They, in turn, perceived her as unfriendly and aloof, though, in fact, she longed for a friend and confidante. She spent much of her day lonely and depressed, facing life with little joy or anticipation of what each new day would bring. While she could talk about her life and memories, she didn't feel she could make new friends now. "This is just the way I am," she declared, "and it is too late to change now!" In fact, sometimes people do report finding new ways to interact with others, but it requires a readiness to try, which Ramona did not have.

Hiring a full- or part-time home health aide can be a superb solution to loneliness if one finds a compatible individual. Earlier we described a childless widow in her 90s who found the right person in a kind aide from Ghana who became her unofficially adopted daughter, to the great benefit of both.

Of course, it can be a disaster if the fit is bad. In either case, many elders are very ambivalent about the idea of hiring an aide who symbolizes for many a waning sense of independence and privacy.

As fewer social interactions occur, life begins to center around doctor visits, which are often the elder's only trips outside their home during a week. These visits can be very positive experiences with a kind and genuinely interested medical team. But if a trusted nurse or doctor gets impatient or annoyed or seems to ignore the elderly patient and instead interacts with a family member or aide, elders may leave feeling resentful and sad. And the stigma many elders already feel of being a burden and worthless is reinforced.

### Social Relationships and Health in Later Years

Keeping up good relationships not only feels good but, as research is telling us, it's a critical component in maintaining physical and mental health, even to the extent of predicting mortality. In order to explore these studies, it's useful to understand the terms used and how they are measured.

- *Social ties*, or *social integration,* are measured by simply counting the number of social ties to family, friends, and organizations.
- *Social isolation* refers to having few social ties; the fewer social ties people have, the more socially isolated they are.
- *Loneliness* refers to the subjective feeling that one's social ties are inadequate or less than one desires. One popular way of measuring loneliness is through

self-report questionnaires, such as the University of California–Los Angeles loneliness scale.

Being able to study people and their interactions more scientifically has spawned a burst of research that has implications for health, as well.

### The Effects of Social Isolation on Health and Mortality

In the 1960s, researchers in epidemiology and sociology began exploring the connections between social relationships and health. In 1988, James House and colleagues reviewed a number of studies that had followed people over a period of years. These studies looked at the relationship between social ties and mortality in places as varied as California, Georgia, Michigan, Sweden, and Finland.

Regardless of where the studies were conducted, the pattern was the same. People who were socially isolated were more likely to die during the period studied than people with more social ties. One study followed 5,000 adults in Alameda County, California, for almost a decade. Researchers gauged subjects' social ties by measuring spouse, family, friends, and organizations to arrive at a social index score. People with a low social index score were twice as likely to die as those with a high score. House and colleagues found that social isolation was as large a risk factor for mortality as cigarette smoking, high blood pressure, obesity, and lack of physical exercise.

Just why this might be is a question we'll discuss soon. First, let's explore the subjective experience of loneliness.

*Loneliness: The Emotional Impact of Perceived Isolation*

Of course, being alone doesn't necessarily feel bad. Some of us prize our solitude and are happy to use it for contemplation or to pursue cherished activities. But, sometimes, people are not just alone, they're lonely and don't feel fine at all. Stories of loneliness can be traced in the literature through the millennia and across many cultures. However, it has been in the last century that scientific research started to focus on the subject. Psychoanalyst Frieda Fromm-Reichmann raised awareness of it in the late 1950s with her seminal paper, "Loneliness."

More recently, technology has ushered in increasingly rapid communication as well as more frequent and more varied kinds of social interactions. However, the concern is that this has been at the expense of more immediately meaningful connections. Sitting, talking, and being together allows us to share ideas in a more personal and intimate way than the Internet and e-mail allow. One grandmother reported a visit from her 15-year-old granddaughter. The exasperated grandma told her charge, "If you don't put that gadget away and talk to me, I'm going to flush it down the toilet!" A surprisingly pleasant and quite lovely conversation followed.

Most of us do not have to look far to see the emotional impact of being lonely for older people. Some estimates suggest that 5 to 15% of the oldest old experience loneliness frequently, as they are more likely to have lost friends and family and to be dealing with potentially isolating medical problems, like impairments in mobility, vision, and hearing. Fortunately, the character strengths and virtues we've been discussing can help. But first, let's look further at the far-reaching effects of loneliness, some of which have only recently come to light.

In the last few years, researchers have been exploring the effects of loneliness on mind and body for people of all ages. The University of Chicago research group led by Cacioppo and Hawkley (2007, 2009, 2010) found that high levels of loneliness can have severe effects on the way we function at any stage in life. As they point out, the discomfort that accompanies the feeling of loneliness likely serves an evolutionary purpose, since survival of the species depends on people's ability to work together. The need to feel connected to others is as vital as our bodies' physical needs. Loneliness is the social equivalent of pain, hunger, and thirst. For an estimated 15 to 30% of people of all ages, it is a frequent state, suggesting the deficit of a basic human need. Its effects can be seen on many different levels, not only on our mental health but on our physical functioning, as well.

In the area of mental health and cognitive functioning, loneliness has long been associated with depression and suicide. Some studies found that loneliness predicted depression one year later. In older adults, Reijo Tilvis and colleagues found that high levels of loneliness at the beginning of the study were related to faster cognitive decline over the next four years. Robert Wilson and colleagues found the same to be true over a period of ten years.

*The Physical Impact of Loneliness*

There is increasing evidence from longitudinal studies that loneliness predicts increased physical illness and mortality, even after taking into account factors like age, sex, smoking, and depression. Loneliness also appears to accelerate physiological aging and to be a risk factor for developing chronic diseases like diabetes, cardiovascular disease, and stroke. In a study that followed women over the course of nineteen years, Cacioppo and Hawkley found that chronically lonely women had blood pressure that was, on average, 16 points higher than that of nonlonely women.

Social psychologist Lisa Jaremka and co-workers found that lonely breast cancer patients were more likely to experience pain, fatigue, and symptoms of depression than nonlonely patients. The lonely group also had higher levels of antibodies for cytomegalovirus, further suggesting a possible relationship between loneliness and the body's immune functioning.

How might social isolation and loneliness contribute to such potentially devastating physical changes over time? Though researchers are still trying to determine what is the cause and what is the effect, they are beginning to uncover the many layers of this fascinating relationship.

### Social Isolation, Loneliness, and Health Behavior

One logical explanation is that lonely or isolated people are less likely to have someone to remind them to take their pills or to look out for them. If Maureen Davis—Honorary Director of her assisted living facility—seemed under the weather, one of her many friends at the facility would be likely to notice and suggest she see a doctor. But that would be less likely for a loner like Ramona. The presence of caring others also keeps us alert to better health practices or ways of finding the best medical help.

Lonely people may also be less careful about health behaviors. Research suggests they are less likely to participate in physical exercise and are more likely to drink, smoke, and be obese.

In addition, Hawkley's and Cacioppo's studies found that lonely middle-agers and older adults reported not only more daily chronic stresses, they experienced the same activities as more stressful and felt less capable of dealing with them than those who were not lonely. Perhaps one reason for this increased stress is a tendency that Hawkley and Cacioppo found: lonely people remember more negative social information about past events than nonlonely people. Further, their behaviors tend to elicit the kind of negative behavior they're expecting, just as Ramona's neighbors in the facility found her aloof and stayed away, leaving her to her newspaper.

Hawkley and Cacioppo theorize that lonely people tend to feel socially unsafe and, either consciously or not, are hypervigilant in scanning their environment for potential or perceived threats. If you remember Ramona, she was sure before she even got to the facility that she wouldn't fit in. Lonely people have also been found to secrete more cortisol than nonlonely people, which would be expected in the case of hypervigilance or increased stress. You may recall from chapter 10 that when increased cortisol becomes chronic, it increases the allostatic load. This might explain the many physical problems that result through cortisol's effects on such areas as immune malfunctioning, which has been found to be related to the development of chronic diseases.

On the positive side, even a little bit of meaningful social contact can go a long way. Psychiatrist Joan Kaufman and colleagues (2004) studied abused children who also had a genetic vulnerability to depression, known as the short SERT gene. She found that contact with a trusted adult outside the home reduced their risk of depression by 80%, even if the visits were as infrequent as once a month.

## WHAT CAN LONELY ELDERS DO TO FEEL LESS LONELY?

There are many potential ways for elders to become more engaged with other people, if they feel up to it (and perhaps even if they don't, which we'll discuss below, too). There's no gold standard and no one-size-fits-all solution. Each person is different, and finding the right approach for any one person takes time and patience. The first step, of course, is to recognize that we're lonely and would benefit from trying to engage the world more. If you know a lonely elder or are one yourself, here are some approaches to recommend or try.

### *Helping Someone Else: The Virtue of Humanity*

One side effect of loneliness is that much time is spent alone, with little to distract us from thinking about ourselves and our unhappy situation. Finding a way to help someone else is a win–win situation. It distracts from our own problems and allows us to reap the emotional reward that comes from helping someone else (not to mention the added benefit for the person we help). If you remember our discussion of the Experience Corps program, volunteering helped elders not only emotionally but also physically and cognitively.

Some of the Vintage Readers Book Club members read to the blind or volunteer at soup kitchens. Some participate in programs in their apartment buildings—affiliated with the national organization Aging in Place, which identifies elders in a particular building whom others can check in on or buy groceries for. Such programs create a smaller, more intimate group within the larger apartment community.

Sometimes, people aren't physically up to the task for a regular volunteer effort. Like 92-year-old Meryl Specter. But Meryl still felt connected to the world, nonetheless. Proud of her ardent liberal politics, Meryl enjoyed contributing to presidential campaigns that she was passionate about and staying up to date on the literature of her favorite causes. Psychologist Elizabeth Dunn's work has shown that spending money on others, regardless of how much it is, actually feels good. Brown and his colleagues similarly showed that for elders, any expenditure, whether it's time, money, or goods, has great benefits both emotionally and physically. The capacity to help others doesn't depend on social status. People with very little money can find the same joys from helping their neighbors as do wealthy philanthropists.

## Helen Bloom

Helen Bloom is an 85-year-old retired nurse who particularly enjoyed being able to help others in a specific and professional way. She worked at the same hospital for fifty years and was beloved by the patients. Even after she retired, she was active in her religious community, where she regularly visited members who were ill, and she conducted a weekly support group for older women, who looked forward to their sessions. She found meaning and purpose in helping others and was happy to be distracted from her own losses due to arthritis and the deaths of dear friends and loved ones.

*Exercise: The Virtue of Temperance*

Elders aren't always like Energizer bunnies when it comes to exercise (and they have a lot of company of all ages), but the mental and physical benefits are so great that it's worth pushing oneself to do it. It is even better if one knows of someone else who might also benefit and can be a companion. Remember the powerful positive effect of social support for both of you. Exercise also helps keep the endorphins flowing, which reduces pain and enhances well-being. Exercise groups for elders are particularly useful because they offer a built-in chance for socializing and making new friends as well as getting us out of a sterile home setting. If it's too hard physically to get to a gym or senior center, having a physical therapist come to the home is a great way to promote a better mood and better health; the therapist can also make suggestions for improving balance in order to help elders prevent falls.

*Taking a Class or Starting a Group: Wisdom,*
*Humanity, Being a Bridge*

It's never too late to learn something. George Dawson became a hero to many by learning to read in his late 90s. As we've discussed, keeping our minds active and alert has been found to be important in many ways. Whether at a senior center, school, or college, taking a class—it could be anything from philosophy to ceramics to tai chi—is a way of meeting others with similar interests, whatever their ages. Someone like Ramona, who assumes she won't have much in common with others, might find an environment like this safer. That's why Nancy, the retired architect in her 60s, hopes to start a retirement community near a college for when she's older. It would be a chance to be near both other elders and students of any age who might enjoy learning the same subjects, not to mention a medical center that could come in handy sometimes.

Another way to combat loneliness is to start a club organized around an activity you already enjoy (for example, through a neighborhood library, YMCA, or other community center), whether the activity is reading, writing, knitting, seeing movies or plays, cooking, photography, or anything else. Having topics to share is stimulating and fun. The Vintage Readers Book Club has been just such an experience for everyone who has joined.

Another possibility is offering to teach a class on a topic you love. Like Eddie Weaver, who organized the engineering department of a local community college long after he retired his physics post, or Judy, Mindy's mother-in-law, a retired public school computer teacher. Judy, now 80, has spent her many years since she retired teaching elders at her senior center how to use computers and iPads and how to become proficient Internet users. Her students are grateful for her guidance, as it helps them keep in touch not only with scattered—though beloved—family and friends but helps them stay up-to-date technologically in a world where every new advance might mean new opportunities for making meaningful connections.

### Caring for a Pet: The Virtue of Transcendence

A pet can help immeasurably in transcending loneliness. We both know—and assume you do, too—many older people who found remarkable solace by having an animal to care for and love—and feel loved by. Pets can feel almost human to us, as they understand our mood and needs. Meeting us at the door, jumping into our laps, sleeping on the bed, crawling under the covers to stay warm—all provide an intimacy that can be very comforting. Betty, 79, said that her reason for getting up in the morning was not to greet the world but to feel her beagle's friendly lick on her face. Loving and feeling loved by a friendly beast can attack loneliness at its root. Laura Slutsky, 63, has two dogs that give her "a purpose and a reason to come home." Kate remembers an afternoon when she was sitting on her sofa, feeling so sad that she started to cry. Her cat came running from across the room—jumping from a chair to a table, then bounding across the floor, jumping to another table, then to the sofa, then onto her lap—so that he could lick her tears.

Pets can help in so many ways. Studies have shown that even something as simple as petting a dog lowers blood pressure and enhances a sense of calm. We can see how helpful pets can be by looking at the incredible proliferation of animal therapies, for example, the dogs that visit hospitalized children and elders in nursing homes and communities with an invariable positive response. Seeing eye dogs have been used for decades to help blind people move about.

Canine Companions for Independence trains dogs to help people with various challenges. For instance, for people in wheelchairs, the dogs open doors and cabinets, pay cashiers, and perform a host of other activities; the organization also trains the people in the wheelchairs to handle their dogs. The dogs can also help autistic children with sensory problems. One mother reported that her son's dog pulled him "out of his own little world" and even helped him to sleep through the night (Heaps 2012). New possibilities are always being found, even horse therapy for adolescents. And for reducing distress, veterans with post-traumatic stress disorder are now given trained dogs to help them control their fears. The United Kingdom has even begun experimenting with dogs to help elders with dementia.

## Pet Love

Joanne and her husband, Sigh, were always "poodle people," and walking their dog three time every day was a ritual that kept them exercising and out of doors. After Sigh's death, Joanne kept up the daily walk of a mile three times a day, which was good for animal and human alike. But even more important was the fact that she met her good friends from the "doggy world" at the dog park and enjoyed this built-in daily resource for socializing.

When apartment buildings do not allow cats and dogs, birds can become the best option. Jimmie recalls one elderly woman who found great joy in the sounds of her singing canary that she loved, petted, and cared for like a child. And there's Mildred and Oscar Larch's cockatiel, Jocko, who ran their home from his perch. Even watching goldfish or tropical fish can provide an aesthetic experience. And being responsible for keeping the fish alive and healthy can have a profound effect on their caretakers. If you remember the Langer and Rodin nursing home studies, even being responsible for taking care of a plant improved the lives of nursing home residents immeasurably.

The care of plants can take on the same meaning as the care of a pet. One elder who was alone, except for an aide, made a point of picking up the discarded orchid plants in her building. She formed an "orchid resuscitation unit" for these discards, which she nursed back to health—and blooms. She says, "They know very well when they are loved."

*Support Via Online Resources: Humanity and the Courage to Learn Something New*

On the one hand, online interactions and social media allow people to keep in contact with each other much more easily than ever before. On the other hand, technology changes so quickly, it's hard for some elders to keep up, and they often end up feeling even more isolated as a result.

It's not just elders. It wasn't that long ago that Mindy asked her toddler to teach her how to use their universal television remote control (so many buttons!). Once her children are out of her home, it will be harder to keep up. The longer she goes without being plugged in to every new change, the harder it will be to take advantage of these changes, and she might fall behind. An elder without an Internet connection might have fewer chances to connect with the outside world than before, as other people will be less likely to use "old-fashioned" methods like telephone calls and the US mail. Unfortunately, today's state-of-the-art technology is tomorrow's dinosaur.

For elders who are not computer literate, a computer class at a senior center (like the one Judy teaches) or one for beginners at a local school can be a helpful place to start. Elders can meet potential flesh-and-blood friends, while they also learn how to connect to virtual friends. There are even virtual support groups for elders. They can be a particular godsend for those who are home bound.

### The MayMoms: Virtual Friends Are Real Friends, Too

Mindy joined a virtual group when she was pregnant with Max. All the women in the group were due the same month—May 1996—and they called themselves the MayMoms. Most of them have never met in person.

Well, it's 2014, and they still keep in touch. When Mindy started chemotherapy in 2006, her "virtual" friends helped her through it all. Some even made her a beautiful quilt—based on her favorite color combination of yellow and black—to keep her warm. Each woman decorated a square, and then one of them sewed the squares together, while another found the batting material. Mindy was bowled over when she opened the box. Even virtual friends can help us in very concrete, real ways.

Computers, in general, can be a good source of stimulation. There is some evidence that computer games, whether they involve words or numbers, might even help maintain memory, though this is open to debate. Bridge, solitaire, and online puzzles and word games can be both stimulating and a welcome distraction. Finishing a puzzle can bring a very pleasant feeling of mastery. And chat rooms and virtual groups add to the potential for finding people interested in similar topics. When Mindy was going through breast cancer treatment, she found such groups to be an invaluable source of both information and support (even if no quilts). Of course, she took care to select sites carefully.

Often, elders turn to younger family members to teach them to use their computers, the way Jimmie could rely on her grandson's Grandma Software. You'll be happy to learn she has since graduated to version 2.0. This might be a fun exercise for everyone. Though, in fairness, there might also be some frustrations involved, and the need for patience on the parts of both teacher and student should be discussed up front. But one possible rallying cry is that if George Dawson can learn to read in his late 90s, then perhaps octogenarians and nonagenarians and maybe even centenarians can give technology education a chance, too.

## WHEN SOMEONE ELSE'S HELP IS NECESSARY TO GET PAST INERTIA

These suggestions are well and good for those who can work up the momentum to give them a try. But what if it's too hard to get past the inertia of staying home or remaining socially isolated?

Lonely elders often resist getting out to make new acquaintances or to try the senior citizen center. Even picking up the phone to inquire about a program may feel like too much effort. They might be suffering from a treatable depression that others will miss, assuming it's just a part of "getting old." But the U-bend data remind us that this isn't necessarily so. We know that that there are many elders who are actually more satisfied with their lives than ever before. Why not strive to be one of them?

This section outlines the range of possibilities of getting help to counter loneliness when we just can't seem to do it ourselves. This intense, heavy kind of loneliness may appear in the context of grief over the loss of a spouse or friend, severe disappointments or regrets from the past, friction with children and other family members, physical disabilities, or by actual depression that you can't seem to shake.

### The First Step Is Recognition

Sometimes, we just know when we're so distressed that we need help. But sometimes, we don't and we assume, as others often remind us, that feeling sad and lonely comes with the territory. In these cases, the front line for identifying the elder in need of psychological help is often in the primary care doctor's office. Many times, it is a perceptive nurse who notices a change in manner. The better the staff know the older person through his or her visits over the years, the more likely they are to pick up on worrying signs, like: "I just stare at these four walls all day." "I wake up and realize there is no reason for getting up." "I am just taking up space and I am of use to nobody on the planet."

A good physician then does a careful physical examination to see if these bad feelings are due to any physical problems that can be treated. It may be important to ask an aide or family member about any observed changes in the elder's behavior. It might be worth making some suggestions for anti-loneliness homework, to find the phone number for the senior center, for example, and call it for information or the number for the local gym for exercise. Jimmie offers an

*A* on her patients' "report cards" for one phone call per day to a friend. It's important to be aware of valuable resources, like schools, gyms, neighborhood art classes, library events, and senior centers. Many cities offer a huge range of opportunities for social interaction and support.

An elder's primary care physician might feel that a referral to a therapist is in order. Today's elders grew up during a time when there was a big stigma attached to anything "mental," and seeing someone for mental health meant you were morally weak. So, they might not wish, at least at first, to see anyone. If they change their minds or trust their doctor's judgment enough to give it a try, it is helpful if the doctor can offer names of several professionals who see older people regularly and can make a personal referral.

Unfortunately, there are all too few professionals around who specialize in the problems of older adults. This is an issue the health care system is just beginning to address, as the number of elders continues to increase. In the meantime, there is a range of mental health professionals who can be helpful. Social workers are often a part of the front-line team; psychologists are sometimes available as well as mental health counselors. Elders who are particularly religious may prefer someone from their faith community who has counseling skills, like pastoral counselors.

Psychiatrists should be available if significant symptoms of depression or anxiety warrant medication. A particular concern is depression, particularly in elderly white men, who have a higher suicide rate than any other group. The more closely the mental health professional is related to the primary care physician, the better, and the more likely the elder will be to follow up. A nearby office—or even better, a mental health person who is on the medical team—provides the best integration.

## COUNSELING ELDERS: THE VIRTUES
## AND CHARACTER STRENGTHS COME IN
## HANDY IN THERAPY, TOO

Cacioppo and Hawkley (2009) did a meta-analysis of the literature on the effectiveness of various types of psychological treatment for lonely people. Their analysis suggested that lonely people's social sensitivity combined with their tendency to remember negative aspects of interactions more than positive ones made them more reluctant to interact with people the next time around. This, in turn, made them less likely to have positive social experiences, which further intensified their reluctance to try, creating a "loneliness feedback loop."

These researchers also found that therapies aimed at helping elders reframe these negative assumptions were the most helpful. For instance, Ramona must have had some positive social experiences at some point that she could be encouraged to remember and to draw on in order to counter her low expectations. Regardless of the therapist's school of thought, what's most important is a therapeutic relationship based on trust and mutual respect. Group counseling might be helpful, but it is not commonly used by lonely people.

Thinking about the character strengths and virtues we've been discussing can be very helpful for therapists as they try to help lonely elders reframe social experiences or just cope with the many losses that often accompany aging. Over the years, Jimmie found it particularly helpful when working individually with the oldest old to mention traditional sounding words like "virtue," "strengths," and "encourage." These are the kinds of words they grew up with and are likely to be more meaningful than modern psychological terms with which they are less familiar and that they sometimes find dubious.

The first step for a therapist—or for friends or family, for that matter—is to listen. Really hear what seems to be troubling the elder and how he is managing it. It's helpful to inquire and really listen to what's going well, too. Difficult challenges come from many places, from a new financial or personal situation, feelings about deteriorating physical abilities, or fears about memory problems. While it's very common for people to have Alzheimerophobia, it can be very comforting to know that most memory problems in older age are due to benign forgetting disorder of older age.

Rather than thinking only about problems, it's important to help the elder think about strengths that can be gleaned from how she has handled past crises or problems and then to apply those strengths to the current situation. We have found it particularly helpful to say something like, "Remember how you have heard all your life about courage—well, you are showing it right now in how you're dealing with this. It is one of the key virtues that man has relied on for millennia." Self-esteem is often battered by aging problems, and support that suggests, "You may be doing a better job than you think!" can go a long way to bolstering self-confidence.

Developing the art of forgiveness may be another way of using the virtues to combat loneliness. Harboring unspoken resentments is a formula for feeling separate from other people. Ruminating can also keep us mired in the past, less able to live in the here and now, which so many elders find essential to *traveling light*. Sometimes, the ruminations aren't about others' wrongs but about elders' own past mistakes, which they can't undo. If the elder can remember times when he has forgiven others and when others have forgiven him, the memory can serve as a model for the present. It can help him forgive himself for past transgressions that can't be changed, and lighten his burden.

Using the virtue of wisdom can be complicated. Our two expert panels of older adults all agreed that they did not like to be referred to as wise. But when it's an appropriate description (as opposed to an empty honorific condescendingly imposed on elders because others assume it makes them feel good), we can remind the elder of the wisdom of particular decisions she made in the past or the wisdom of particular insights she gleaned from her experiences or from dealing with current dilemmas. Being reminded of deserved praise can help bolster self-esteem and optimism that a new challenge can be met equally well.

Also, reminding people of the transformative effects of becoming more aware of the little joys and pleasures of the day can help elders consciously open themselves up to experience transcendence. Dorothy Kelly, for example, found that meditating in the corner of her room for fifteen minutes every morning gave her the strength to begin the day and do the things she needed to do. Helping younger women in business or in Alcoholics Anonymous was a similar transcendent experience that kept her from feeling lonely and was enjoyable in and of itself.

### The Phone

The telephone remains a critical tool of communication for many elders, whether receiving calls or calling for help, if needed. The comforting sound of another person's voice is not easily replaced by e-mail. As we described in the Introduction, Jimmie's geriatric psychiatry team developed a phone-based counseling model for older adults. The sessions focus on such issues as reviewing their lives, looking at their strengths over the years, reframing problems so as to tackle them in a better way, and addressing loneliness. So far, preliminary data suggest that these techniques help counter loneliness and encourage better coping.

Doctors who care for many older patients may be surprised to find that even a simple check-in phone call once a week has a surprisingly big impact. In a large study of older patients receiving chemotherapy for cancer, psychologist Alice Kornblith and colleagues found that a monthly phone call to monitor how the patients were coping reduced anxiety and depression. Interestingly, when patients were asked what they found helpful about the calls, they said, simply, "Somebody cared about me between my monthly doctor visits." Similar to Kaufman and colleagues' 2004 study, such a simple intervention—a little social support—goes a long way to make an older person feel better.

### Medications

Many older people dislike taking yet another pill, often for good reason. Sometimes it's their long list of medications and their side effects that contribute to their feeling sad, lonely, and depressed. Sometimes, just pruning unnecessary medications or lowering doses can improve their mood. Other times, adding a psychotropic medication might help. Even if they might be helpful, the rule of thumb for physicians is to start low, go slow, and follow up to ask about any side effects in order to get the most benefit. Sometimes, it's the combination of medication and counseling that is most effective.

Whether for emotional, psychological, or medical reasons, we do better when we're as socially connected as we want to be. And, even when we aren't as connected as we'd like, contrary to our assumptions in the past, our brains and bodies are capable of more dynamic changes than we ever guessed. While it is hard to totally change our social environment, just tweaking it a little can have a big impact on how we feel.

## REFERENCES

Barger, S. D. (2013). Social integration, social support and mortality in the US National Health Interview Survey. *Psychosom Med,* 75(5), 510–517.

Burmeister, S. S., Jarvis, E. D., and Fernald, R. D. (2005). Rapid behavioral and genomic responses to social opportunity. *PLoS Biol*, 3(11), e363.

Cacioppo, J. T. and Patrick, W. (2009). *Loneliness: Human Nature and the Need for Social Connection*. New York: W.W. Norton.

Creswell, J. D., Irwin, M. R., Burklund, L. J., Lieberman, M. D., Arevalo, J. M., Ma, J., Breen, E. C., and Cole, S. W. (2012). Mindfulness-based stress reduction training reduces loneliness and pro-inflammatory gene expression in older adults: A small randomized controlled trial. *Brain Behav Immun*, 26(7), 1095–1101.

Dawson, G., and Glaubman, R. (2000). *Life is Good*. New York: Random House.

Dobbs, D. (2013, September 3, 2013). The social life of genes. *Pacific Standard*.

Fromm-Reichmann, F. (1959). Loneliness. *Psychiatry: Journal for the Study of Interpersonal Processes*, *22*(February), 1–15.

Giervel, J. d. J., van Tilberg, T., and Dykstra, P. A. (2006). Loneliness and social isolation. In A. P. Vagelisti and Perlman, D. (eds.), *Cambridge Handbook of Personal Relationships*. Cambridge: Cambridge University Press, 485–500.

Hawkley, L. C., and Cacioppo, J. T. (2010). Loneliness matters: A theoretical and empirical review of consequences and mechanisms. *Ann Behav Med*, *40*(2), 218–227.

Hawkley, L. L., and Cacioppo, J. T. (2007). Aging and loneliness: Downhill quickly? *Current Directions in Psychological Science*, *16*, 187–191.

Hawkley, L. C., Thisted, R. A., Masi, C. M., and Cacioppo, J. T. (2010). Loneliness predicts increased blood pressure: 5-year cross-lagged analyses in middle-aged and older adults. *Psychol Aging*, *25*(1), 132–141.

Heaps, S. (2012, December 3, 2012). Service dog, boy with autism are likely best friends, web. *The Daily Herald*. Retrieved from http://www.heraldextra.com/news/local/south/spanish-fork/service-dog-boy-with-autism-are-likely-best-friends/article_c72a2824-a7e0-53ae-8241-2e1f6b25dcea.html

House, J. S., Landis, K. R., and Umberson, D. (1988). Social relationships and health. *Science*, *241*(4865), 540–545.

Jaremka, L. M., Fagundes, C. P., Glaser, R., Bennett, J. M., Malarkey, W. B., and Kiecolt-Glaser, J. K. (2013). Loneliness predicts pain, depression, and fatigue: Understanding the role of immune dysregulation. *Psychoneuroendocrinology,* *38*(8), 1310–1317.

Kaufman, J., Yang, B. Z., Douglas-Palumberi, H., Houshyar, S., Lipschitz, D., Krystal, J. H., and Gelernter, J. (2004). Social supports and serotonin transporter gene moderate depression in maltreated children. *Proc Natl Acad Sci U S A*, *101*(49), 17316–17321.

Kornblith, A. B., Dowell, J. M., Herndon, J. E., 2nd, Engelman, B. J., Bauer-Wu, S., Small, E. J., Morrison, V. A., Atkins, J.,

Cohen, H. J., and Holland, J. C. (2006). Telephone monitoring of distress in patients aged 65 years or older with advanced stage cancer: A cancer and leukemia group B study. *Cancer*, *107*(11), 2706–2714.

Langer, E. J., and Rodin, J. (1976). The effects of choice and enhanced personal responsibility for the aged: A field experiment in an institutional setting. *J Pers Soc Psychol*, *34*(2), 191–198.

Masi, C. M., Chen, H. Y., Hawkley, L. C., and Cacioppo, J. T. (2011). A meta-analysis of interventions to reduce loneliness. *Pers Soc Psychol Rev*, *15*(3), 219–266.

Slavich, G. M., and Cole, S. W. (2013). The emerging field of human social genomics. *Clin Psychol Sci*, *1*(3), 331–348.

Tilvis, R. S., Kahonen-Vare, M. H., Jolkkonen, J., Valvanne, J., Pitkala, K. H., and Strandberg, T. E. (2004). Predictors of cognitive decline and mortality of aged people over a 10-year period. *J Gerontol A Biol Sci Med Sci*, *59*(3), 268–274.

Wilson, R. S., Krueger, K. R., Arnold, S. E., Schneider, J. A., Kelly, J. F., Barnes, L. L., Tang, Y., and Bennett, D. A. (2007). Loneliness *and risk of Alzheimer disease. Arch Gen Psychiatry*, *64*(2), 234–240.

Yalom, I. D. (1980). *Existential Psychotherapy.* New York: Basic Books.

# 13

# The Virtue of Appreciating the Cycle of Life in Elders

*... were it offer'd to my choice, I should have no objection to a repetition of the same life from its beginning, only asking [for] the advantage authors have in a second edition, to correct some of the faults in the first.*
    —Benjamin Franklin, *The Autobiography*

*Old age ain't no place for sissies.*
    —Bette Davis

Ben Franklin expressed what most elders feel: they would take the same life again, even if they might prefer to omit a few faults the second time around. "I am still ME," they seem to be saying. "Surely, I did not live a perfect life, there are regrets, but it was the best it could have been, given the cards I drew." We see in them an acceptance of life and of their responses to it. All the virtues we have been discussing are brought to bear in the elder years, just as in the younger years. But, for elders, there is often something additional. As noted by philosopher William May: "When [virtues] do appear in the elderly,. . . they can instruct and sometimes even inspire. Their example can encourage the fainthearted among the young who believe that full human experience is possible only under the accidental circumstances of their own temporary flourishing" (1986, 50).

## AGEISM AND HISTORY

When we began thinking about this project, we were particularly impressed by the work of Robert Butler, the founder of the National Institute on Aging, who coined the word *ageism* to describe the American culture's romance with youth and beauty and its negative attitudes toward aging. Millions flock to their plastic surgeons so as not to look like "those old people." In fact, aging is often thought of as a nonstop time of disability, deterioration, and death. Of course, no one can deny that disability and deterioration come with the territory for many people, though not for everyone. Death, of course, ultimately does come with the territory for everyone. But, as we've been discussing, these facts are not the whole story, not by a long shot.

Coupled with this stigma is the notion that old people are taking up space and money. Many younger people would prefer not to see elders nor be reminded of aging, and would prefer segregating them into their own communities. Some feel it is all right to demean them and make fun of their foibles. Though elders may join in and laugh about the consequences of aging with the kind of shrug that just says, "It is what it is."

We feel it's important to educate the younger generations about their attitudes (and where they come from, but more on that soon), but it's also important to remind elders that they don't have to see themselves in the same harsh terms, like Lillian, who didn't start to feel old until "other people started treating me like I was old." As Vintage Reader Anne-Marie said, "I think we cause our own problems by buying into these ideas in the first place."

We have to wonder why ageism and gerontophobia—the fear of aging or of older people—have managed to survive through the millennia. One would have to assume that these negative attitudes reflect something much deeper than a fear of wrinkles or loss of hearing, to have taken such a strong hold over our imaginations across so many generations, despite the remarkable changes in the world since ancient times.

## Fear of Aging as a Fear of Death

Perhaps aging is particularly frightening because it is viewed by the young as the last stop on the train before death, as Cicero pointed out. We don't want to think about death, and so, aging, too, must be denied or avoided at all costs. It's easy to keep from facing our mortality when we're young and life seems endless. A young woman who had a serious illness once told Jimmie, "I know I am going to die, but I can't believe I'm going to die." It was incomprehensible that one day she might not *be*.

Awareness and acceptance of mortality are gradual processes. Usually, the first death a young person experiences is that of her grandparents, who are often close enough that their loss touches her, but distant enough that the loss is emotionally tolerable. A national survey found that almost half of us begin middle age with both parents alive, whereas three quarters of us leave middle age having lost both parents. Mindy is fortunate enough to still have both parents, ages 90 and 78. But, in general, as adults reach middle age, they begin to recognize that if nature follows its normal course, they likely will face the death of their parents.

This moment was a particular turning point in Jimmie's life. She had felt "safe" as long as her parents were alive. With the death of her second parent, she thought, "Now, there's nobody left between me and the grave." Watching our parents age reminds us of the approach of death. We may start to experience anticipatory grieving that one day they will be gone. And we are reminded that we ourselves are, as Scipio tells Cato in Cicero's essay, "travelers who mean to take the same long journey" (211).

### The Eternal Quest for Eternal Life

For all the information about the inevitability of death, stories of immortality—how it just might be possible—are centuries old and continue to this day with great popularity. Despite the reality, people still seek nostrums that promise the death of death, in books, television shows, and movies. The ancient Sumerian epic of Gilgamesh is among the oldest surviving works in literature. Told 1,500 years before Homer and older than the Bible, it is a story of the grief of King Gilgamesh following the death of his friend, Enkidu. Gilgamesh seeks to overcome death, win back his friend's life, and secure immortality for himself, as well. He almost succeeds.

The gods tell Gilgamesh he can find eternal life if he eats a plant that lives at the bottom of the sea. Gilgamesh weights his legs with stones and finds the plant on the ocean floor. He then cuts the ropes from around his legs, releasing the heavy stones, and rises to the surface with the plant.

But Gilgamesh isn't the only one who wants the plant's magic. When he gets to shore, he leaves the plant temporarily unattended while he goes off to retrieve water from a nearby well. He returns to find that a serpent has eaten the plant, leaving behind its shedded skin. Defeated, the king falls to the ground and weeps, while the snake, having sloughed off its old skin, begins its new life.

The serpent has remained a symbol of regeneration and immortality and became associated with Asclepius, the ancient Greek god of healing and medicine. He is famously depicted with a staff at his side on which a snake is entwined; the rod of Asclepius has been associated with the healing arts of medicine ever since. At one of the early temples of Asclepius in Pergamum, the Greeks carved a serpent into the side of one of the pillars at the entrance. The serpent can still be seen today on the pillar's remains. It is said that the priest kept nonpoisonous snakes on the floor as a symbol of hope, regeneration, and immortality.

Legends about a spring that restores the youth of anyone who drinks or bathes in it have existed for thousands of years, including one described by Herodotus, and the Water of Life sought by Alexander the Great. In sixteenth century Europe, many such popular tales inspired explorers like Ponce de León, who was believed to have stumbled onto Florida as a result of his search for the Fountain of Youth. St. Petersburg, Florida, where he is said to have first landed, celebrates the story as part of its tourist attractions. While, today, we might ridicule a belief in magic fountains, many believe the advertisements for death-defying and anti-aging creams, vitamin, and elixirs, instead. It is safe to say that the wish for immortality remains alive and well.

### *Appreciating the Life Cycle*

This brings us back to the question of why the U-bend shows greater well-being in elders who are closer to death than their younger counterparts. It is counterintuitive. Yet, interestingly, it validates the observations of Cicero, as does our own experience: older people are not, as a rule, morose or terrified of death. Like Lillian says, "When I was very little, I was terrified of death. Now, I'm not overtly terrified. I'm annoyed. I want to see what happens next."

Physician and philosopher Lewis Thomas thinks about this new understanding and acceptance in universal terms:

> *We will have to give up the notion that death is cata-strophic, or detestable, or avoidable, or even strange. We will need to learn more about the cycling of life in the rest of the system, and about our connection to the process. Everything that comes alive seems to be in trade for some-thing that dies, cell for cell. There might be some comfort in the recognition of synchrony, in the formation that we all go down together, in the best of company.* (99)

Yes, older people may make their wills, choose their health proxies, and talk about funeral plans. But these are the steps of appropriate planning. Some would add that doing these things actually makes elders feel better—making plans, seeing to it that their children won't be burdened, and selecting a trusted person to be at their side. Besides, when these things are done, they put aside the topic and go back to living in the now. Rather than denying the reality, they live with it.

## Tuck, Everlasting

*Tuck, Everlasting*, a children's book by Natalie Babbitt (2007), provides an interesting perspective on death and the desire for immortality. Tuck, his wife, and two sons inadvertently drink from a magic spring that protects them all from aging and death. Each remains the same age as when he or she drank the potion, despite the passage of years and years. Sooner or later, the sons have to give up their relationships because the women they've married continue to age normally, while they remain young adults forever. The family has to move because neighbors start to realize that there is something strange about them.

When a young girl named Winnie finds the magic spring, she prepares to drink from it. Tuck warns her not to and describes agelessness as a terrible burden. He explains that watching life is like watching a flowing stream of water. The stream continues but always with different water. And that is the same as the rest of nature. "Winnie, the frogs is part of it, and the bugs, and the fish, and the wood thrush, too. And people, but never the same ones. Always moving in the new ways, always growing and changing and always moving on. That's the way it's supposed to be. That's the way it is." When Winnie says she doesn't want to die, he answers, "But dying's part of the wheel, right there next to being born. You can't pick out the pieces you like and leave the rest. Being part of the whole thing, that's the blessing. . . . You can't have living without dying" (62–64).

Elders get it: life is what it is, and they come to live with that reality as a given fact. They don't dwell on it. Instead, they put it aside to make the most of each day they have. This ability is one of the greatest lessons they offer the rest of us. And this so-called children's book should be on all adults' bookshelves.

For "seasoned elder" Joan Lustig, the notion of immortality—or living longer—was scarier than the idea of death.

## Joan Lustig: Saved by Her Accountant

Joan was a vibrant 89-year-old widow who had no children and little company, as most of her friends had died. She prided herself on her frugality, and managed to adapt to retirement, widowhood, and even ovarian cancer quite well. She had always lived alone, but she liked her solitude and felt well despite the various aches and pains of aging.

However, a visit to her doctor changed all that. He told Joan that her heart problem was at a point that it would likely progress in the coming months and that she should organize her life accordingly, while she was still physically able to deal with it. He suggested that she move to assisted living.

Overwhelmed by the idea of losing her home, Joan became acutely depressed. She decided to explore having an aide come to her home instead and found someone she liked very much. But could she afford to pay her? How long before her money ran out, and what then, when her savings were gone?

Joan had a trusted accountant to whom she turned for advice. Based on his calculations, he said, "Joan, you can keep this lovely lady you found for the next 19 years!"

Her fears abated, and she laughed as she announced she was financially safe, at least until the age of 108. For Joan, it was the fact of her mortality that was reassuring, when what she feared most was outliving her money.

### Reality, but a Broadened Perspective of Self

In general, the recognition of mortality brings to mind the need for all the virtues to help us cope with this scariest part of life—like courage, and the shared experience of humanity. As the Blade Runner realized about his enemy, "All he'd wanted were the same answers the rest of us want. Where did I come from? Where am I going? How long have I got?" (*Blade Runner*). "We all go down together in the best of company, Lewis Thomas said. The closer we are to contemplating mortality and death, the greater the need to muster the best parts of ourselves.

One of Jimmie's favorite passages comes from Fannie Flagg's book *Welcome to the World, Baby Girl*, set in a small Missouri town that recalls the rural scenes from Jimmie's youth. In Flagg's book, Aunt Elner, whose whole world consists of her immediate environs, puts the big existential questions in a simple context:

> . . . *Poor little old human beings—they're jerked into this world without having any idea where they came from or what it is they are supposed to do, or how long they have to do it in. Or where they are gonna wind up after that.* **But bless their hearts, most of them wake up every**

**morning and keep on trying to make some sense out
of it.** *Why, you can't help but love them, can you? I just
wonder why more of them aren't as crazy as betsy bugs.*
(448; bold ours)

Indeed, "trying to make some sense out of it" is what
we all do, while managing to put one foot in front of the
other every day, and keep going. It may be that accepting the finiteness of life—like a deadline out there when
you are younger—spurs us to take care of more important things and to "not sweat the small stuff." Laura
Carstensen and her colleagues have studied the impact
of shortened time perspective and found that the sense of
a shortened time to live contributes to the greater sense
of well-being. For Nancy, a large part of the equanim-
ity that came with later middle age was due to her ability to accept living with uncertainty about the future. It
allowed her to better appreciate the present moment in
time, feeling less burdened by yesterday and less worried
about tomorrow.

A foreshortened time span means less need to please
others or to worry about career goals and our children
who are largely on their own. The big burdens of the
middle years are indeed behind us. The knowledge that
there's a lot less time in front of us than behind us often
leads to greater concern about our personal relationships.
This concern, in turn, can lead us to try to repair fractured
or neglected relationships. For philosopher William May,
it's the proximity to death that fuels our need for transcendence, so that we can put our mortality in a larger, more
meaningful context: to forgive and be forgiven; to have a
sense of contentment and purpose; to stop and enjoy the
way the sunlight streams through the streets when you're

looking in just the right direction; to appreciate a moment of beauty such as a glorious piece of music or a beautiful sunset. It's a little like tidying up loose ends and truly being able to live and appreciate each moment. In other words, *traveling light*.

### Gratitude and Humor

The limited time perspective also contributes to a sense of gratitude in older people for having lived for many years, and even for life itself. As we discussed in chapter 6, humor becomes particularly important; it enables us to make light of the hassles and discomforts of daily life in our older years. Grace and grit are equally there, tinged with joking about the infirmities. At one of our group meetings when the conversation became devoted to a description of the physical symptoms that was too detailed, one member commented, "We don't need an organ recital here."

### Telling Us What to Pack

The special attention given to people who speak out about their terminal illness suggests that people want to know more about what it feels like to be facing death. It is as if people facing it have some special knowledge to impart to the healthy and the young. But it's best heard if sprinkled with humor. An example is Morrie Schwartz, a retired professor at Brandeis University who had amyotrophic lateral sclerosis (ALS), a fatal disease with progressive loss of muscle strength.

## Tuesdays with Morrie

Sportswriter Mitch Albom reached out to his old teacher Morris Schwartz after Morrie became a national figure thanks to his interview on the news show *Nightline*. Morrie, a teacher for more than thirty years, chose to use his death as his final teaching project: "Learn with me," he tells Mitch, who immediately signed up for the class *Morrie 101*.

"Mitch," he says, "people see me as a bridge. I am not as alive as I used to be, but I am not dead. I'm sort of . . . in between. I'm on the last great journey here and people want me to tell them what to pack. . . . Once you learn how to die, you learn how to live."

Morrie, like Lewis Thomas, points out that we're a part of nature. But he goes further. Because we're also different from the rest of nature—we can understand and we can love.

"As long as we can love each other, and remember the feeling of love we had, we can die without ever really going away. All the love you created is still there. . . . Death ends a life, not a relationship." (174)

Aging is not only about the abilities we lose over the time, but the insights we gain. On the fear of growing old, Morrie feels, "you understand you're going to die and you live a better life because of it."

## Art Buchwald: "Celebrity for Death"

Another celebrity who used his approaching death to teach about it—with uncommon good humor—is

Art Buchwald, longtime syndicated columnist and humorist. "Dying isn't hard," he said, "getting paid by Medicare is hard!" (9). Like Morrie, Buchwald found people were very happy to share their questions and fears about dying.

Ironically, while Buchwald thought of himself as a "celebrity for death," he became famous for putting death on hold for a while. So long, in fact, that he was kicked out of hospice and sent back home. He had first entered hospice when he was 81, because his kidneys weren't expected to last more than a few weeks. He left five months later, still going strong. He received letters and phone calls from all over the world; people told him that they loved talking to someone who wasn't afraid to discuss death.

"I have to be honest," Buchwald said about being a celebrity for death, "I've enjoyed every moment of it" (89). He went on to write a popular book about these experiences, *Too Soon to Say Goodbye.*

Also like Morrie, Buchwald invited his friends to celebrate his "living funeral" so that he could enjoy it with them rather than having to be absent. He had them send him their eulogies for him, so he could include them in his book. *Washington Post* editor Ben Bradlee wrote, "He made everyone sound interesting and funny, even when they weren't."

On January 17, 2007, almost a year after Buchwald thought his death was days away, the *New York Times* ran a video of him beaming as he announced, "Hi, I'm Art Buchwald. And I'm dead!"

### The Last Word

People who face their mortality in the here and now often have a sense of what their lives have meant to them, and they wonder what their lives will have meant to the people around them. Usually, they have in mind many of the qualities we've been discussing. Art Buchwald, for instance, wanted to be remembered for being able to make people laugh, as he told the *New York Times* for their video series, *The Last Word*. Other prominent people interviewed for the series also had strong feelings about how they wanted to be remembered and seemed happy to discuss it.

For newsman Mike Wallace, 88, it was to be thought of as "tough but fair." For baseball player Bob Feller, it was as "a kid from a family, who had great parents, great coaches and teachers, and loved his country." Buchwald actually has three videos rather than the usual one; as his status as a celebrity for death grew, people wanted to hear from him more, not less.

Elders can teach us many things, by example, about facing life and death. Their greatest obligation as mentors to the younger generation is to help them understand, as Cato did in Cicero's essay, that old age is not as bad as you think it will be, death is not something to fear so much, and, above all, not to let either of them get in the way of living. Elders live with this reality and often thrive in it. The more younger people can interact with them, informally and honestly, the greater the chance to lessen the young's fears of mortality and aging; most elders would welcome the chance to talk about the experience, as we can both attest.

Children's book author Maurice Sendak's final lesson for National Public Radio interviewer Terry Gross and her audience could not have been more clear about the lesson he wanted to pass on: "Live your life, live your life, live your life."

## REFERENCES

Albom, M. (1997). *Tuesdays with Morrie: An Old Man, a Young Man, and Life's Greatest Lesson.* New York: Doubleday.

Anonymous. (1960). *The Epic of Gilgamesh: An English Verison with an Introduction.* Sandars, N. K., Trans. Vol. Tablets 11, 12. London: Penguin Classics.

Babbitt, N. (2007). *Tuck Everlasting.* New York: Farrar, Straus and Grioux.

Buchwald, A. (2006). *Too Soon to Say Goodbye.* New York: Random House.

Butler, R. N. (2008). *The Longevity Revolution: The Benefits and Challenges of Living a Long Life.* New York: Perseus.

Carstensen, L. L. (2006). The influence of a sense of time on human development. *Science, 312*(5782), 1913–1915.

Carstensen, L. L., Pasupathi, M., Mayr, U., and Nesselroade, J. R. (2000). Emotional experience in everyday life across the adult life span. *J Pers Soc Psychol, 79*(4), 644–655.

Cicero, M. T. (1820). *An Essay on Old Age.* Translated by W. Melmoth. Google Ebook.

Flagg, F. (1998). *Welcome to the World, Baby Girl!* New York: Random House.

Franklin, B. (1961). *The Autobiography and Other Writings.* New York: Penguin.

May, W. (1986). The virtues and vices of the elderly. In T. R. Cole and S. A. Gadow (eds.), *What Does It Mean to Grow Old: Reflections from the Humanities.* Durham, NC: Duke University Press.

McDonald, B. (2012, April 8, 2012). Last word: Mike Wallace. *The New York Times*. Retrieved from http://www.nytimes.com/video/obituaries/1194826917764/last-word-mike-wallace.html

McDonald, B. W., T. (2007, January 18, 2007). Art Buchwald: I just died. *The New York Times*. Retrieved from http://www.nytimes.com/video/obituaries/1194817093353/i-just-died.html?playlistId=1194820770698

Orr, M. (2010, December 15, 2010). Last word: Bob Feller. *The New York Times*. Retrieved from http://www.nytimes.com/video/obituaries/1247464008751/last-word-bob-feller.html

Sendak, M. (2011). On life, death, and children's lit. In T. Gross (ed.), *Fresh Air:* National Public Radio.

Thomas L. (1974). *Death in the Open Lives of a Cell: Notes of a Biology Watcher* (pp. 96–99). New York: Viking.

Warren, R. (1998). *Women's Lip: Outrageous, Irreverent and Just Plain Hilarious Quotes*. Hysteria.

# Appendix

# Vintage Readers Book Club Readings

*The Autobiography of Benjamin Franklin*, Dover Thrift Edition, 1996, selected passages

*Essay on Old Age* by Marcus Tullius Cicero, 44 BC, translated by W. Melmoth

Discussion of Virtues:
> "The six universal virtues," from *Character, Strengths and Virtues* by Christopher Peterson and Martin Seligman, Oxford University Press, 2004
>
> Benjamin Franklin's list of thirteen virtues, from *The Autobiography and Other Writings*, Penguin Group, 2001

*The Apology* by Plato, circa 400 BC, from *Man and Man: The Social Philosophers*, 1947, edited by Saxe Commins and Robert N. Linscott, Random House

*Travels in Cancerland: Make Your Garden Grow*, 2012, written and published by Reva Greenberg

*Letter From Birmingham Jail,* Martin Luther King, Jr., 1963
*Declaration of Independence*, Thomas Jefferson, 1776
*The Meditations of Marcus Aurelius Antoninus*, 2nd century, selected readings from Books I to V

Discussion of Humor:
> *Viva la Repartee*, 2005, Dr. Mardy Grothe
> *Archy and Mehitabel*, Don Marquis, 1927/1987, Anchor edition
> Miscellaneous readings recommended by group members

*Abraham Lincoln's Second Inaugural Address,* 1865

Plutarch's *Letter of Consolation to His Wife*, first century

"Hope is a state of mind, not of the world," by Vaclav Havel, from his book, *Disturbing the Peace*, Knopf, 1990

*You Learn By Living: Eleven Keys for a More Fulfilling Life,* Eleanor Roosevelt, 1960, Harper

*Aesop's Fables*, selected readings

Discussion of Memory:
> Passages from St. Augustine's *Confessions*
> "Personal memory and the biology of memory storage," from *In Search of Memory: The Emergence of a New Science of Mind* by Eric Kandel, 2006, Norton

Discussion of Walt Whitman:
Selections from *Leaves of Grass*
*A Backward Glance O'er Traveled Roads*

The Fight for Women's Rights in U.S. History:
*Eyewitness To America*, edited by David Colbert, Pantheon Books, New York 1997
*Witness to America*, edited by Douglas Brinkley, Harper Collins Publishers, 1999, 2010
*The Women's Rights Convention* (Seneca Falls, NY 1848)
*Forty Years at Hull House*
*United States vs. Susan B. Anthony*
*Raid on An Abortion Clinic*
*The Feminine Mystique and the Women's Rights Movement*
Selections from The Complete Poems of Emily Dickinson, edited by Thomas H. Johnson. 1960, Little, Brown and Company:
#254, 1129, 288, 1212, 712, 1478, 308, 578, 441, 143, 1438

# Index